THE HUNTER'S GUIDE TO
PREPARING AND COOKING GAME

A HANDBOOK OF PRACTICAL TECHNIQUES: HOW TO DRESS AND COOK GAME IN THE FIELD, WITH 30 CLASSIC RECIPES

ROBERT CUTHBERT AND JAKE EASTHAM • RECIPES BY ANDY PARLE

southwater

This edition is published by Lorenz Books,
an imprint of Anness Publishing Ltd,
Blaby Road, Wigston, Leicestershire LE18 4SE

Email: info@anness.com

Web: www.lorenzbooks.com; www.annesspublishing.com

If you like the images in this book and would like to investigate using
them for publishing, promotions or advertising, please visit our
website www.practicalpictures.com for more information.

Publisher: Joanna Lorenz
Editorial Director: Helen Sudell
Executive Editor: Joanne Rippin
Food styling: Fergal Connolly
Photography: Jake Eastham
Butchery: Ray Smith
Locations: Stowford Manor Farm: www.stowfordmanorfarm.co.uk
and Brokerswood Country Park: www.brokerswoodcountrypark.co.uk
Props styling: Julia Meadowcroft
Designer: Nigel Partridge

ETHICAL TRADING POLICY
Because of our ongoing ecological investment programme, you, as
our customer, can have the pleasure and reassurance of knowing that
a tree is being cultivated on your behalf to naturally replace the
materials used to make the book you are holding. For further
information about this scheme, go to
www.annesspublishing.com/trees

NOTES
• Bracketed terms are intended for American readers.
• For all recipes, quantities are given in both metric and imperial
measures and, where appropriate, in standard cups and spoons.
• Follow one set of measures, but not a mixture, because they are
not interchangeable.
• Standard spoon and cup measures are level. 1 tsp = 5ml,
1 tbsp = 15ml, 1 cup = 250ml/8fl oz.
• Australian standard tablespoons are 20ml. Australian readers should
use 3 tsp in place of 1 tbsp for measuring small quantities.
• American pints are 16fl oz/2 cups. American readers should use
20fl oz/2.5 cups in place of 1 pint when measuring liquids.
• Electric oven temperatures in this book are for conventional ovens.
When using a fan oven, the temperature will probably need to be
reduced by about 10–20°C/20–40°F. As ovens vary, check with your
manufacturer's instruction book for guidance.
• The nutritional analysis given for each recipe is calculated per
portion (i.e. serving or item), unless otherwise stated. If the recipe
gives a range, such as Serves 4–6, then the nutritional analysis will be
for the smaller portion size, i.e. 6 servings. The analysis does not
include optional ingredients, such as salt added to taste.
• Medium (US large) eggs are used unless otherwise stated.

PUBLISHER'S NOTE
Although the advice and information in this book are believed to be
accurate and true at the time of going to press, neither the authors
nor the publisher can accept any legal responsibility or liability for any
errors or omissions that may have been made nor for any
inaccuracies nor for any loss, harm or injury that comes about from
following instructions or advice in this book.

Hunting and shooting seasons, laws and regulations concerning the
purchase or procurement of quarry species vary from country to
country, and state to state, and must be adhered to. In no way are
the publishers or authors responsible for any breaches of these laws.
Permits\licenses must be obtained in line with the specific regulations
of the country you are in, and permission from the landowner should
always be obtained. Disposal of offal and waste should be done
responsibly and in line with regional health and safety regulations.

Contents

Introduction

The purpose of this book is to provide the hunter and cook, whether a novice or experienced, with a practical guide to making the best use of the game birds and animals that are available to us. Detailed sequences show how to butcher the different species, and the wonderful recipes will be an inspiration to all those who want to cook this wonderful food outside.

THE HUNT

Even though we no longer need to hunt and shoot wild creatures for food, many still choose to do so, preserving our sporting traditions and heritage. The history of the pursuit of animals for food is very long. It is clearly charted in prehistoric cave paintings, and there is strong evidence from the Mesolithic period, around 8000BC, to suggest that animals were chased into pits or steered over cliff edges by groups of hunters long before developments in flint-knapping techniques enabled effective spears and arrows to be made.

The hunter-gatherer societies of pre-history followed rules and rituals associated with the hunt that still have

▼ *One of the best ways to enjoy fresh game is to prepare it and cook it in the wild, where it belongs.*

▲ *Few other pastimes leave the tired but happy sportsman with some of the tastiest, healthiest foods available.*

echoes in game shooting today. Those new to modern wing-shooting or stalking are often beguiled by the sport's rules of etiquette, safety, customs and dress. Indeed, especially across France, Belgium and Eastern Europe, detailed post-hunt rituals are often as important as the hunt itself. Bonfires are lit and mournful tunes are played on large brass horns by men resplendently dressed in dark green loden coats and

feather-studded hats, and emotions rise as the lament is played over the animals taken that day. This proclaims thanks and respect, to the animal and to the chase itself, as does the Scottish rough shooter carefully removing his pair of prized woodcock's pin feathers, or the Slovakian hunter plucking small branches from a pine tree growing near the spot where his boar or deer fell. Short or protracted, such traditions ensure that the protagonist connects with the quarry and its environment, as well as cementing the camaraderie of a sport that extends across the globe.

GAME PREPARATION

From the moment your shot is taken and your quarry brought to hand – or from when you leave the butcher with your purchase – you'll be able to refer to this guide, which will steer you through the seemingly daunting process of preparing all the major quarry species pursued today. It includes the field evisceration of deer, boar and wild goat, so you can begin to think about how best to prepare the kill even before you've set off for home.

Suggestions for the ideal hanging times are also included. Light hanging is advocated for game birds – probably one to two days and always somewhere very cold and fly-proof. Game needs only a little time to relax and develop flavour, and over-hung or 'high' game can be offputting for those not accustomed to its taste. However, deer need to hang for longer, as you'll discover.

Quarry birds differ from country to country or state to state, but the basic principles are the same, and you will be able to adapt the instructions given for the particular birds included in the book as needed. As you prepare more game and become more competent and confident, you'll realize that with a little adjustment to cooking times, a golden plover, say, will work better in most snipe recipes than woodcock. Similarly, the meat from an axis buck could be a perfect substitute for fallow and red, but works less well for roe deer, and so on.

The job of plucking birds, skinning animals and preparing them for the pot is something both hunter and cook should take pleasure and pride in. This guide will give you the initial burst of confidence you need to take on the job yourself, rather than relying on a butcher to do it, or worse still, wasting the game completely. The birds and animals we're privileged to take for sport can only really be honoured by our subsequent efforts in the field and in the kitchen while preparing them for the enjoyment of our friends and family.

COOKING GAME

The hunter will have to make the best use of whatever he or she happens to shoot. For those buying game rather than hunting it, there is plenty of guidance on what to look for and how best to cook it at home. Game dealers and butchers are themselves a hugely underused resource when it comes to the slightly intimidating prospect of choosing suitable game for the pot, so do seek their advice.

The lone pot-hunter, out for a day in the field with a dog and a few pigeons in the bag, may be looking for a change from those flash-fried breast fillets. Rabbit, squirrel and pigeon are good examples of game that can be easily found, shot and cooked in moments with the minimum of fuss but maximum

▼ The recipes in this book include modern takes on classic dishes as well as enterprising new ways to cook game.

enjoyment. Bag staples like pheasant and partridge blend beautifully with autumn vegetables, while true residents of the forest, like the woodcock, are perfectly partnered with fungi such as porcini, morels and oyster mushrooms.

COOKING IN THE FIELD

Each chapter contains detailed butchering sequences for each type of game, followed by wonderful recipes that have been adapted to cooking in the field. Cooking and eating outside is a joy, especially for the hunter, and an open fire is surprisingly easy to cook on. Many of the recipes can be cooked successfully on a camp fire, with the wood smoke flavouring the dish and the fresh air sharpening the appetite, others can be cooked on a barbecue. Whether you are cooking out in the wild, in your own back garden or in the kitchen, this collection of dishes will inspire you to extend your enjoyment of eating game.

▲ It is much easier than you might think to cook truly fabulous food outdoors, and with game as the centrepiece you will be sure of a great meal.

▼ What better way to end a successful hunt than by cooking on a camp fire?

HUNTING & COOKING GAME

Whether you pick up your pheasants in the market, shoot rabbits in the garden or control deer as a full-time job, this book will help you prepare and cook game in the most efficient way possible. The idea of taking the life of a bird or animal as part of a sporting endeavour is an uncomfortable one for some, but others believe that killing animals as and when they are needed for a meal is a much more ethical way of providing food for the table than intensive farming practices. For the true hunter there is no finer way to honour the lives of these beautiful birds and animals than careful preparation and cooking for the delight of our friends and families. If it is to be your first foray into the hunter's world, these pages offer solid guidance.

◄ *The star of the show. A bird pot-roasted over an open fire with herbs and root vegetables makes a superb evening meal for a night spent camping out, following a successful day in the field.*

A History of Hunting

Cave paintings, friezes, tapestries, sculpture and paintings have all helped historians to chart the development of hunting, from its prehistoric importance as a means of survival, through its use as a foundation for learning warrior-like skills, to becoming the sport of the aristocracy and finally to its modern-day status as a cornerstone of today's rural economy. As exquisitely engraved shotguns and double rifles are bought for vast sums, let us not forget that these are essentially tools: flint axes, spears and arrowheads were the forerunners to longdogs, hounds, falcons, the invention of explosives and ultimately shotguns and rifles.

THE HUNTER-GATHERER

Hunting is certain to predate *Homo sapiens,* the human race as we know it now. The first hunters probably walked the earth about 2.5 million years ago, just as the Ice Age was becoming established. Hunting and gathering food were essential activities for these early communities, not only ensuring survival but also providing elementary social

▼ *A deer brought to bay with bows and arrows – medieval weapons not far removed from those of early hunters.*

cohesion. Prehistoric man lacked the powerful jaws needed to tear meat and so required the help of tools. By 1.5 million years ago *Homo erectus*, 'upright man', was able to craft efficient hand axes and had mastered fire, which revolutionized food preparation.

Around 200,000 years ago, *Homo sapiens* began a slow spread out across the globe from the cradle of humanity in southern Africa. Archaeological finds suggest that early clubs and spears,

▲ *The lifestyle choices of today are born out of the prehistoric era when hunting was necessary for human survival.*

together with more sophisticated tools, were being widely used around this time. The remains of animals closely resembling elk, deer, rhino and mammoth suggest that these were part of Stone Age man's staple diet. It was at this time that domesticated dogs became an established part of hunting.

▲ In the Middle Ages royal decrees barred all but the high nobility of the land from hunting prized game.

Dogs were probably used to assist in early herding tactics, such as steering and harrying animals over cliff edges or into pits.

The formation of farmsteads and the domestication of animals for food was a relatively recent development, beginning around 10,000 years ago, but the ritual of the chase and the dependency on game as a staple food continued to be hugely important.

THE CLASSICAL ERA

Aristocratic Greeks and Romans devoted much of their time to breeding hunting dogs and training them to flush out and worry animals, such as wolves, bears and even lions and other large cats. For the higher echelons, hunting was for sport and status rather than food, but for ordinary people it remained an important way to supplement an otherwise restricted diet. The hide, bones and sinews of many animals were used for clothing and tools.

THE MIDDLE AGES

During the latter part of the medieval era in Europe, up to the 16th century, hunting saw the introduction of strict laws concerning game. As a pastime, it was considered a vital part of the life of the sons of the nobility, improving not only horsemanship but also skill at arms and courage. As a sport, it was enjoyed only by the upper classes; indeed, commoners found guilty of hunting illegally met with the most gruesome of punishments. Branding, castration, blinding and even death awaited those found guilty of poaching. In some countries, the convicted poacher was given the chance of fleeing into the forest, but he was dressed in bloodied animal skins and had to take his chances with the aggrieved landowner's dogs, which were released to pursue him after a short head start.

Hawking and falconry, using birds of prey to bring down rabbits and birds, were very popular medieval pursuits, and this rather genteel aspect of the sport attracted many noblewomen. Deer and boar were pursued on horseback. Although deer were usually dispatched

with bows and arrows, boar were killed at dangerously close quarters, using long staves and spears. Making the fatal blow at the close of a boar hunt brought the hunter great praise and renown. In some areas of Europe, bears and wolves were also pursued for sport, safety and to protect livestock.

▼ A romantic image of a poacher. The penalties levied on those found guilty of this crime were disproportionately harsh.

▲ *King Edward VII (centre) inspecting the bag at Sandringham, Norfolk, 1909.*

HUNTING WITH FIREARMS

Although it is well documented that unsophisticated artillery was used by Chinese gunners in the 11th century, it was not until towards the end of the 13th century that gunpowder really began to find popularity with national

▼ *After a day in the field on a private estate, there's still the enjoyment of the post-shoot analysis and dinner to come.*

armies worldwide. The subsequent development of sporting guns was simply a spin-off from this revolution. The skills employed to build field cannon were refined to make portable versions: the crudest forms of matchlock-activated, muzzle-loading guns came into existence, primarily from the east, around the late 1400s.

THE EARLY MODERN ERA

From the late 13th to the 15th century, birds were shot above dogs, using flintlocks and similar 'fowling pieces', which succeeded the earlier matchlocks. The flintlock model lasted, with only minor refinements, well into the 1820s. However, in the second half of the 19th century the dynamic was to change in such a way that shooting game would never be quite the same again. Stalking for deer, wild sheep, goats and boar continued, with only the refinement of the rifle and the development of the telescopic scope after World War I being worthy of any note, but driven game became hugely popular among the upper classes. Its boom coincided with the breech-loading, hammerless shotguns with ejectors, which were in use by 1890.

THE EDWARDIAN ERA

It was in the Edwardian age that shooting parties became the rage among Britain's highest society. At these extravagant events, lavish meals were

▲ *King Christian of Denmark (left), in traditional shooting apparel, and Crown Prince Frederick in military uniform at a formal shoot in 1938 on the island of Seeland, a wildlife haven in Denmark.*

served as musical quartets played, and thousands of birds and hundreds of hares and rabbits were killed each day. Britain was far from holding the monopoly in excess, however. The Spanish nobility under the leadership of King Alfonso XIII, together with Hungarians, Germans and even Bohemians, followed suit with relish.

Figures like King Edward VII, Kaiser Wilhelm and Archduke Franz Ferdinand shot thousands of birds in a single day, giving rise to the notion that the birds were pretty unchallenging targets. However, one has only to examine the game registers and diaries of these men to discover that with the occasional assault on snipe or grouse they often shot dozens of birds without missing once – a tremendous feat even today.

After World War II the breaking up of vast private sporting estates became widespread in Europe, necessitated by death duties and taxation. Slowly this began to provide opportunities for the rest of the population to hunt and shoot, both for sport and for the table.

SHOOTING TODAY

Hunting is now a much more democratic activity, and is enjoyed around the world by many different groups of men and women. These days a single rifle, or a team of guns, can find the type of hunt they crave, in any country they prefer, book it through the internet and enjoy it in all its glorious forms. Many private estates now quietly open their doors to paying customers, and there is rough shooting to be had on farmland in most countries.

Modern shooting comes with a fairly heavy amount of responsible self-governance and regulation, which, on the whole, rests fairly easily with the shooting community. Bag sizes are generally more judicious, the nurturing and shooting of small bags of wild birds for eating grows in popularity and, overall, a more accountable, caring and longer-term view is being advocated.

As lovers of game and the enjoyment of hunting, it is important for us to stress that a responsible and sustainable approach to shooting for the pot is vital. We can then pass on the sport's heritage to future generations and ensure that they will have the same opportunities as we have today to participate in a sport that has been enjoyed for thousands of years.

▼ *The rough shooter, found the world over, finds happiness in walking a wood or skirting a hedge-lined ditch.*

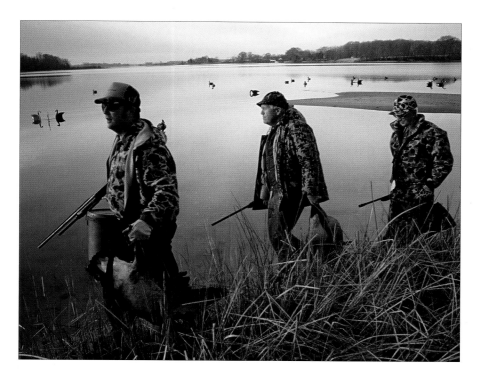

▲ *Decoying for geese is an inexpensive and thrilling sport for the wild bird enthusiast, which can pay dividends in both size and flavour.*

SHOOTING IN EUROPE

Rough shooting in all its forms continues to thrive across Europe, and rifle hunting or stalking is as popular as ever, while boar shooting has exploded in popularity over the past decade.

Driven bird shooting in countries such as Slovakia, Hungary and parts of Scandinavia seems to grow steadily, both in demand and in the quality of the experience provided. Aristocrats and newly wealthy sporting families have often sampled driven birds in Britain and seek to emulate the British approach to the sport, offering high-curling birds. Castles, mansions and other impressive homes are increasingly becoming backdrops to sporting house parties, with the quality of the birds' presentation becoming more significant. Elaborate post-shoot ceremonies and celebrations are a strong draw for clients from the United States and Britain.

USA AND CANADA

Although Canadian and American shooting parties have become part of the fabric of British and European shooting, they have their own sporting challenges at home. Like most American sportsmen, the Canadian gun shoots pheasant, grouse, partridge, chukar, quail and wild turkey. Goose and duck shooting, in all their forms, are also tremendously popular. As in many other countries, responsibility regarding the number of wild birds taken in a day has increased dramatically in recent years.

▼ *With blaze-coloured apparel, a father and son return after pot-hunting. Shot birds are carried by the feet in the US.*

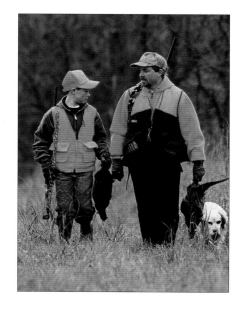

Modern Hunting Methods

Whether rough shooting, stalking or taking part in a formal drive, there are several ways to source your own game. Here are some of the most widely used.

DECOYS AND HIDES

One of the most popular forms of shooting is not strictly for a game bird but for an agricultural pest species – the ubiquitous wood pigeon. Although these birds are widely written off as vermin, they still – like the truly wild species that inhabit rivers, lakes and coastal areas, such as geese and wildfowl – have a strong role to play within the sport and also in this book.

These incredibly wary birds can be shot coming in to roost at dusk, but by far the most popular way to shoot them is by way of decoying: the birds are shot having been attracted in close to the pattern of decoys. Until the last second, the shooter conceals himself behind a hide, which may be a mesh curtain or a purpose-built cover of camouflage fabric, positioned close to the crop the pigeons have been feeding on. Store-bought hides are usually upgraded with twigs and foliage to help them blend in.

Crops such as peas, beans and certain seeds are irresistible to pigeons.

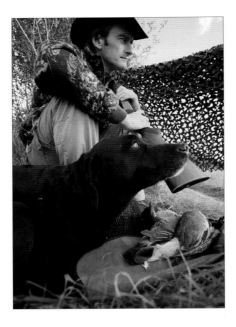

▲ *Pigeon shooting in a hide needs a quick eye and a sure, steady aim.*

With a little reconnaissance to determine established flight lines, the shooter can get himself a spot among large numbers of these challenging targets. Given the right conditions, a well-sited formation of pigeon decoys will provide the sportsman with a truly bountiful day. Decoys may be either recently shot real

birds propped into lifelike feeding positions, or plastic shells that mimic the bird's most obvious characteristics of matt grey colouring with distinctive white collar feathers and bars on each wing.

A relatively modern innovation in this sphere is the introduction of the 'pigeon magnet', which is essentially a large battery with a number of protruding arms, on which dead pigeons are mounted with their wings outstretched. The central motor rotates the birds in an extremely lifelike manner. Such machines have a real ability to catch the eye of these suspicious birds and attract them into the shooter's arc of fire. Purists dismiss them as unsporting gadgets. So they may be, but when numbers count they are considered vital to the dedicated pigeon controller.

Bags running into hundreds of birds, shot by a lone gun, are far from unusual; although this can seem crass and greedy to the uninitiated, it can't be emphasized strongly enough that pigeons are an absolute menace to arable farmers. Flocks can ravage crops in a matter of hours. Guns who regularly shoot large numbers of pigeons often have standing arrangements with local game dealers to make sure no birds are

▼ *Calling ducks and geese into your decoy pattern is an art. The wrong call could send every single bird away.*

▼ *Decoying wild ducks takes fieldcraft, patience and warm clothing. You may spend hours waiting, but it's worth it.*

▼ *Decoying for pigeons is a wonderful and inexpensive way to obtain some fantastic shooting.*

▲ *This Canadian duck hunter has the first one of this flight in the bag.*

wasted. Most, however, will want to keep a few for themselves, as they are truly delicious.

Wild ducks are decoyed in a similar fashion, with plastic replica ducks floated and anchored on lakes or coastal inlets. Ideally, leading ducks spot the decoy ducks already settled on the water and follow them in, only to be ambushed by the waiting gun. Wild ducks are not really considered pests, and the reduced bags reflect this fact. Indeed, many countries impose strict limits on some wildfowl and geese shot.

Traditional duck hides tend to rely on more natural materials than pigeon hides, utilizing waterside reeds and rushes, but where ducks are driven or flighted often and seen in great numbers, duck-shooting organizers and estate owners often build permanent hides or blinds. It isn't at all unusual even to have floating blinds as permanent fixtures, usually in the middle of vast lakes. Again, with a nod to the locale, these blinds are often made using natural materials such as reeds, which not only work beautifully in concealing the shooters, but blend in far more naturally than anything artificial. Keen wildfowlers are a hardy breed and their quarry recognition is usually second

to none; it has to be. Often shooting in half-light, they need to be able to pick out and ignore protected species in favour of something delicious like the widgeon, the mallard or the highly prized and diminutive teal.

ROUGH SHOOTING

This covers a wide range of informal forays for the hunter – and often for his or her dog. It could just as easily be a freezing excursion after a few skulking ptarmigan, cautiously picking your way over icy rocks on glacial foothills, or flighting a few woodcock along an avenue of firs under a huge full moon before you start to prepare dinner. The combinations and variations are as endless as the fantastic opportunities offered, so long as permission has been obtained and the necessary documents and insurance are all in place.

With few limitations in terms of cost, organization and dress code, for a group of friends, or indeed a solitary shooter working through cover with a beloved dog, rough shooting is truly wonderful sport and a terrific way to harvest a more eclectic selection for the table. The joy, excitement and sheer thrill of never really knowing what you may encounter makes this form of the

▼ *The rough shooter needs little more than a gun to acquire a meal.*

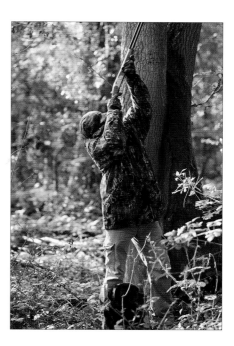

▲ *As a wood awakes or begins to settle, a still and silent gun waits for a shot.*

sport incredibly popular. Fieldcraft plays a fundamental role in rough shooting. Moving quietly and looking for signs of feeding or droppings can give the shooter an edge in surprising something tucked into a grassy tussock or hedge.

Don't forget that the wonderful countryside can also have a huge bearing on the dishes that are ultimately produced. A rabbit bagged in an orchard brimming with apples and pears offers a superb combination. A brace of partridges may be put up by a pointer and sent tumbling into kale or cabbages, both vegetables that can work beautifully with these toothsome little birds.

With a day's rough shooting, the whole process can be seen through from beginning to end. Working a spaniel through some kale, sugar beet or an expanse of boggy marsh can literally start a meal there and then. A lucky left and right may provide an early couple of snipe for the bag, and a hare would be a lovely surprise too. If there's already a pheasant in the freezer, a nice duck found on the wander back home would make just the right mix for a casserole or terrine. Rough shooting is nature's supreme lucky dip of both sport and food source.

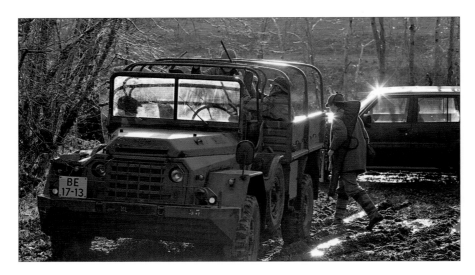

FORMAL DRIVEN SHOOTING

Today, all but a few historic European private estates rely on the letting of driven shooting to offset the costs of the family's sport or to help finance the running of a large estate. Non-shooting landlords also offer sporting rights, and together with farmers wandering their own lands, co-operatives and the formation of paying syndicates, there are plenty of opportunities for people to claim something wholesome and inexpensive to eat from the land.

Some private estates that nurture small stocks of wild partridge and pheasant will cull predatory vermin and cultivate the perfect wild-bird habitat by building beetle banks, or leaving large

▼ *The beaters, pickers-up, flag men, 'stops' and the chef are all important for a formal shooting day to succeed.*

▲ *On a driven shoot the day begins early after a hearty breakfast.*

areas unpolluted by pesticides to encourage insect life – pivotal for the initial protein spurt required by young, weak chicks. This cultivated paradise has the added benefit of boosting and attracting a far healthier stock of other wildlife to the area, as well as providing a thriving habitat for songbirds. Estates of this kind in France and Britain certainly shoot far fewer birds than commercial shoots but, for them, less is definitely more. Admirably, in parts of France grants have even been made available to encourage shoots to nurture wild birds in preference to released birds. With farms and shoots offering both wild and stocked birds, the enjoyment of driven shooting is also growing vigorously in the United States.

Formal driven shooting involves the principal guests, or 'guns', standing in a slight horseshoe shape, or line, roughly 15–30m (50–100ft) apart, facing a wood or a block of cover crop: this may be maize, kale or even roots like turnips and Jerusalem artichokes. With driven grouse, the guns wait in sunken hides known as butts, which are positioned in lines across the moor.

The estate's head keeper, the man responsible for the running of the day, will then order his team of beaters, armed with stout sticks or flags, to walk steadily forward, tapping their sticks on trees and cracking their flags, through the rough cover towards the team of waiting guns in the distance. On some estates, highly regimented beaters make no sound other than the tapping of their sticks, whereas other shoots are happy for their people to cluck and whistle or shout, 'Hi, hi, hi,' 'Yay, yay, yay,' or 'Allez, allez.' Children new to the beating line love the noisier option, thrashing bushes with sticks.

Some shoots and estates also use working dogs like Labradors and spaniels to help flush the birds out of the dense cover, up and towards the waiting guns, in what is referred to as a drive. There are usually four to six drives in a day, lasting from 15 minutes to an hour or more. The aim is to have a constant stream of birds flying in twos

▼ *With a trip booked probably several months ago, the anticipation at the beginning of a shoot is high.*

▲ *The tools of the beater's trade: flags to crack and sticks to beat with. It is said that hazel has the most resonance.*

and threes over the guns, ideally at a height of around 30–40m (100–130ft). Of course, the beating line can be hundreds of metres away from where shots are taken, but all those shooting will have been given a safety briefing.

The most popular venues for driven shooting are historic estates, castles and châteaux, simply because these establishments often have a solid sporting pedigree, with decades of experience. Very often the estates have the appropriate organization and topography to ensure that the birds

presented to the waiting guns are of the finest quality. In short, they are very difficult to shoot – often curling and as high as 60–70m/200–230ft or more: an attractive challenge to the skilled marksman or markswoman.

Not surprisingly, the price of a day taken at such an estate is considerable, but the quality of the sport will be beyond question. Bags are usually paid for in advance, days of 100–300 birds being the norm. The cost is usually worked out on a 'per bird' basis, and depends on the quality and the reputation of the estate or shoot.

To some extent, the public image of shooting game as corporate entertainment still carries the scars of

▲ *Red grouse, driven over guns in Yorkshire, England: the most high-octane aspect of driven game shooting.*

the 1980s, a time perceived as one of colossal bonuses and brazen excess. Although the damage is slowly being repaired, and the lust for large bags reminiscent of the Edwardian era is fading, for the captains of industry shooting remains a popular business and networking opportunity. The traditional shooting fraternity may criticize this, but it is imperative that novices are encouraged and their skills nurtured, as they will help to ensure that game from the field is kept on the menu in both home and restaurant.

▼ *Wellington boots are essential wear in muddy conditions, but on grouse moors, boots and gaiters are preferred.*

▼ *Little can match the elegance and handling of a traditional pair of English side locks.*

▼ *Where shooting is concerned, tradition is rarely far from the surface, and the wearing of tweed is still popular.*

COURSING

Although most of the species covered in this book will be brought to hand by way of a shotgun or a rifle, some hunters enjoy the sport of coursing with dogs to provide them with something tasty for the table. However, it must be stressed that coursing is illegal in some countries, and it is imperative that the law is both understood and adhered to with regard to any coursing activity. In those countries that still allow it, the art of pitting a speedy dog against rabbits, hares and sometimes deer remains hugely popular.

Coursing is one the oldest hunting methods and it survives today in differing forms. Pests like wolves, foxes and coyotes were once hunted this way, but now dogs are usually matched for sport, singly or in twos and threes, against rabbits and hares, or even deer and similar animals for the table. There is a school of thought which argues that some animals will release a significant amount of natural chemicals into the body when chased by hounds, resulting in flesh that is rendered too tough for the table. If you find this to be true, experiment with hanging times and marinades to redress the problem.

Lurchers are the devastating combination of sight hounds such as greyhounds and whippets – renowned for their pure speed – with Bedlington or other terrier breeds for sheer tenacity. The lurcher is a dog type rather than a breed, and is thought to have been introduced during the Middle Ages. While those in the upper classes ran pure-bred sight hounds like wolfhounds, borzoi, salukis, Afghans and greyhounds, the lower orders sought their own hunting dogs. As poaching on

▼ *Even a lurcher has difficulty matching the stunning turn of speed achieved by a wild hare in flight.*

▲ *The distinctive profile of a lurcher shows its lean physique; bred for hundreds of years for speed and agility.*

land owned by royalty or the nobility carried the severest of penalties, it was imperative that a lurcher did not in any way resemble a pure-bred hound. For if a peasant had indeed owned such a hunting dog, he would be presumed to be a poacher and a thief and might be banished, branded or even put to death. A slightly scruffy, broken-coated lurcher, which could assist on the farm and bring home the odd rabbit, was a prized and popular animal indeed, although its owner still often trod a fine line with the local landowner.

STALKING

Although many refer to it simply as hunting, we define stalking as the pursuit of four-legged mammals with a rifle. Of course, foxes and other vermin are shot with rifles too, but in this book we are concentrating solely on bounty for the table.

Whether the quarry is a red deer taken after an exhausting and wet crawl through streams and heather in an icy wind, or a wild goat on a sun-bleached,

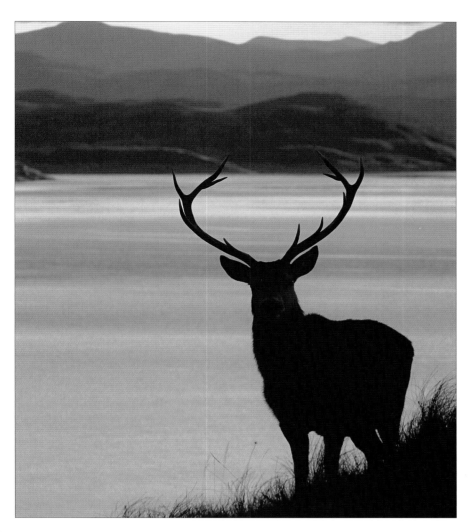

◀ *A red stag in all his glory. A day in pursuit of the mighty red is a serious mental and physical challenge.*

host, only for him to lower the rifle, flick on the safety catch, and smile as the fleeting opportunity is happily, deliberately, lost.

It is interesting that very often someone who has never experienced a day in the field of any description will express the idea that placing a round through an area the size of a splayed hand offers no great challenge at all. However, the ideal scenario, when accompanied by a guide or professional stalker, is to make the best use of the wind conditions and the surrounding topography and cover for the shot to be taken at a reasonable distance, say 60–120m (200–230ft). So, although in essence the beast may be only 1,000m (3,280 ft) away when targeted, the stalker may have to crawl and slither many times that distance in order to get into position for the shot, completely undetected. Rest assured, by the time the rifle is in position, the stalker is cold and wet, with lungs bursting with the effort, and placing that shot is not so easy. If the shot is true, then the work towards the table can begin.

▼ *Moments from the quarry, this stalker edges closer to his deer; surely, the ultimate pressure shot.*

rocky hilltop, the animal is usually hard won after hours of pursuit. Because of this, the stalker perhaps enjoys the fruits of his labour more than the driven game shot; maybe the hours of walking, crawling and imposed silence seal a bond between the hunter and the hunted, ending not just after the trigger is squeezed, but when the knife and fork are placed on an empty plate.

Unlike formal driven game shots, who will be part of a team shooting hundreds of birds in a day, rifle shots are often quite happy to strike out on a freezing cold day, get soaked to the skin and yet still not manage to bring the rifle to the cheek. The exercise can be enough reward when it is combined with the connection of utter solitude amid breathtaking scenery. It is far from unheard of for a guest rifle to be offered the chance and privilege of taking a trophy stag, as a gift from a generous

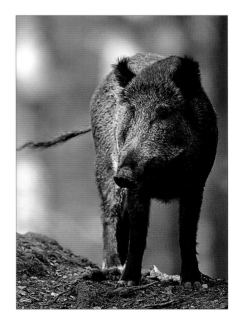

▼ *The boar's secretive habits offer few opportunities for the hunter, but once brought to hand it is worth all the risks.*

SMALL FEATHERED GAME

Game birds, like wildfowl, are an incredibly healthy source of meat protein, with hardly any natural fat. Because of the free-roaming and constant grazing nature of birds, their diverse diet results in a depth and inimitability of flavour not found in farmed or intensively reared poultry. When you consider the plethora of insect life, seeds, berries, grains and fallen fruit that birds feed on, it's no wonder that game provides such an extraordinary, unrivalled assortment of deep and piquant flavours. Birds like partridge, quail and those real prizes, the snipe and the woodcock, can all be cooked in moments, with the minimum of fuss and equipment; all you need for a fabulous meal is your field-fresh bird and the wonderful recipes found in this section.

◄ *An early morning hunt, which bags several birds, can provide a whole day of eating in the field, with flash fried tender cuts followed later by a flavoursome casserole.*

Plucking a Small Bird

The sequence below shows the plucking of a grouse, but you can follow the same procedure for any small- to medium-sized bird. The best position to take when plucking is to sit on a chair, with a cloth or dish towel over your knees and a bin between your legs. Keep your fingers slightly damp as you work, as it gives you more purchase and grip. A wet cloth draped over your knee or shoulder is an easy way to do this.

▶ *With a little hanging, a grouse will pluck just a bit more easily.*

1 Place the bird breast down with its tail end nearest you. Close to the top of the neck, smartly pull or cut the head off and discard it into the bin below.

2 First pluck the base of the bird's neck, removing small bunches of three or four feathers at a time. Be careful of any yellow areas: these indicate seams of fat where the skin tears easily.

3 Holding the bird breast down, move on to the back and shoulders, still plucking the feathers in small clusters. If there is too much resistance, you've probably grasped too many feathers.

4 Moving on from the shoulders, pluck the wings, but only to the first joint you reach. Cut through the tendon hinging the first wing joint.

5 Remove the wing tip, complete with feathers, and discard it. Repeat with the other wing. (If you wish, you can retain and freeze all the wing tips you remove during a season and use them, once plucked, for stocks and gravies.)

6 Once the back is clear of feathers, move on to the legs, keeping contact with your hands to a minimum to help keep the bird's temperature as low as possible. This will reduce the chances of any spoiling.

7 Turn the bird over on to its back. Secure the bird in one hand, gripping with your fingers either side of the wishbone at the neck end or just below the rib section. Start to pluck the underside of the wings.

8 Move on to pluck the whole breast area. Keeping your hands away from the breast will keep the meat cool.

9 Turn the bird so its tail is now farthest from you, but still breast-uppermost (with smaller birds you can pin the legs back using your thumb) and pluck away the smaller feathers from around the vent area.

10 Singe off any stray hairs by passing the bird through the flame of a gas burner, on a low setting.

11 Take a moment or two to pick off any remaining stray feathers or 'cat hairs' that are still attached.

Feathers as Trophies
A quickly plucked feather is often a first-ever trophy. The tiny pin feathers from a woodcock's wings are often tucked into the band of a sporting hat. For centuries, these dart-shaped feathers were sought after by painters of miniatures as paint brushes, for the highly detailed work they helped to achieve.

▶ *The plucked bird ready for drawing.*

Preparing Teal

Although it is widely considered the finest eating of all the wild ducks, the flavour of teal is very similar to that of the partridge in that it offers a good entry-level experience of eating game for the young or uninitiated. The slight downside, of course, is that teal are not as easy to come by as the humble mallard. For that reason, teal young or old, male or female, should be seized upon and relished at every opportunity. They are difficult to source from butchers and dealers as they are a cherished addition to any gun's bag.

For the simplest preparation, you need little more than one bird for each person, well seasoned and basted in plenty of butter, then roasted for around 15 minutes at 230°C/450°F/Gas 8. You can colour them to your liking in a pan first if you wish.

Cooking teal in an over-rich, fruity sauce can overcome the bird's delicious flavour; instead, try serving a lighter berry or rhubarb compote as an accompaniment to roast teal.

▶ *These beautifully coloured little birds have such delicacy of flavour that it's worth every minute taken to pluck and prepare them properly. Like the woodcock and snipe, they are a rare delight for the game lover.*

1 Wash the feet, or snip them off. Holding the bird on the board, back uppermost, run a knife tip up the centre of the back of the neck towards the head. Cut off the head and discard it.

2 Holding the neck skin and the crop in the left hand, pull the neck away from the crop and skin. Cut through the skinned neck stump and throw it away, or reserve for stock or jus.

3 Carefully separate the windpipe from the skin of the neck. Stretching the windpipe and gullet, cut through this as close to the bird's body as possible.

4 Push a finger through and into the cavity where the neck was; twist your finger around to release the tissues connecting the organs to the bird.

5 Turn the bird on to its back. Pinch the skin at the tip of the breastbone, above the vent, and cut down halfway through, exposing the intestines.

6 With your knife tip, carefully cut around the vent, leaving this area intact. Take your time doing this part, to ensure nothing is spilt on to the meat.

7 Push a finger into the cavity and remove the contents in a smooth action.

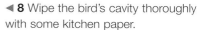

◄ **8** Wipe the bird's cavity thoroughly with some kitchen paper.

9 If drawn properly, there should be no necessity to wash the cavity out, but if you suspect that the gut may have been punctured it's probably wise to rinse the inside of the bird thoroughly under cold running water. Pat the bird dry with kitchen paper, inside and out. If you haven't already done so, remove any stray 'cat hairs' with a lit taper or the gentle flame of a gas burner.

▼ *If you fillet out the teal's breasts, fry them quickly so they do not dry out.*

Tips for Cooking Teal
• The teal is a member of the duck family, and rancid duck fat will ruin a decent bird, so it's important to prepare early-season birds you've shot as soon as possible.
• No member of the duck family needs to be hung, but you might want to leave them for a day to allow the fibres to relax.
• Freshly diced apples, or dried fruit such as prunes and dates, soaked in your favourite tipple – Armagnac, Schnapps or sloe gin, perhaps – work well as a stuffing for any of the smaller birds like teal and the tufted duck.

◄ *Any bird instantly looks a little more presentable with its legs trussed. It also helps the cooking process.*

Preparing and Filleting Wood Pigeon

Wood pigeon is wonderfully inexpensive for both sport and food. It offers a myriad of opportunities for the cook, from a warm salad with the breasts seared for just a minute or so each side, to perhaps a smoked bird eaten cold with pickles and mayonnaise. The combinations are almost endless with this ubiquitous agricultural pest, and the cook certainly shouldn't feel too guilty about using only the breast fillets, as there is very little flesh on the bird's legs. The legs can always be used in stocks and jus.

The pigeon's accessibility, together with its robustness and depth of flavour, means that one shouldn't hold back from strong flavours when cooking it – it is similar to beef in this respect. If you're assured of a few beautifully plump, tender young squabs, then pigeon is delicious simply roasted, one bird for each diner.

Before filleting you will need to pluck and draw the pigeon. The kidneys will still be inside the bird, on either side of the backbone.

▶ *The wood pigeon is a bird that's easily sourced from markets and game dealers, as it is shot in considerable numbers throughout the world.*

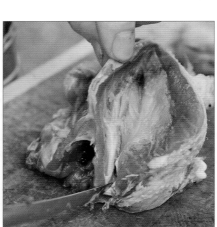

1 Draw and clean the bird as shown on the previous pages. Beginning at the tail end of the wood pigeon, use the tip of the knife to slice down against the breastbone, using the edge of the bone and the hard membranes to guide you.

2 At the bottom of the wishbone, cut through this small tendon and gently ease the fillet away in one piece, making small cuts with your knife.

3 Lay the fillet skin side down to work on its grainy, more textured side. Remove the mini-fillet by gently chiselling out the tendon anchoring it to the fillet. Use gentle strokes, following the natural line of the sheet of tendon.

4 If you intend to use the mini-fillet, remove the other tendon running the length of it, by anchoring the tendon and pushing the flesh away from you with the flat of the knife blade.

5 On the textured side of the large fillet, you'll notice a slightly pearlescent, shiny patch towards the blunter end of the fillet's diamond shape.

6 Carefully cut out this patch of flesh, which leads to the tendon, working from the outer edge inwards.

Tips for Cooking Wood Pigeon

• Empty the bird's crop as soon as possible if you are shooting over rape, clover, peas or other green crops. The contents can quickly taint the flavour of the meat. It is not enhanced by hanging at all.

• If shooting pigeon in the winter months, beware of pea-like ivy berries. They are poisonous. Ensure they are completely removed from the crop area.

• When selecting birds for simple roasting, look out for those that have yet to develop the distinctive collar of white feathers around their neck. Birds without the collar will be fairly youthful, perfect for frying and roasting, and shouldn't need casseroling.

• Pigeon carcasses, well roasted and browned in the oven, make a superb rich stock.

• The pigeon eats peas voraciously, so what better way to cook your pigeon than the French way – with fresh peas, poached in a little water or light stock with some sliced shallots, finely shredded lettuce, butter, sugar, mint, chervil, parsley, salt and pepper.

• If you are roasting pigeon, serve it with potatoes fried in beef dripping and Béarnaise sauce.

7 As you do so, you'll find the shiny patch is attached to a sheet of very tough tendon. Gently scrape the meat away from this and draw it out. Take a little care so you lose hardly any meat.

8 The removal of this 'flight' tendon ensures that the fillet stays flat when cooked. No matter what you do to a fillet that retains this tendon, it will not tenderize. It takes seconds to remove it.

9 To butterfly the fillet, run your knife horizontally through it, starting at the thickest point of the diamond.

10 Do not cut all the way through. The fillet is now ready for cooking.

Preparing and Trussing Woodcock

The woodcock's large probing bill helps it to an opulent diet of worms, snails, slugs, larvae and other protein-rich morsels. This ensures that its flesh is one of the richest, most recognizable of all game birds prepared for the table, with a faintly liver-like quality – once tried, it is never forgotten. This unique flavour is not one to be trifled with; to the purist, anything other than simple roasting with the assistance of a little fatty bacon is regarded as sacrilege.

The traditional method is to roast the woodcock undrawn, with only the gizzard removed. The neck is plucked and the head is skinned. The long beak is then used to skewer the bird, keeping it neatly trussed and tidy during cooking.

When cooked, the tiny brain, like a pearl of pure essence of woodcock, is rightly considered a delicacy. Of course, as with any other bird, woodcock can also be enjoyed drawn and served without the head.

▶ *The much-admired woodcock offers half as much flesh as a partridge, but what there is, is simply delectable.*

Skinning the Head

Some of the most traditional recipes involving this delicious little bird involve utilizing the beak as a skewer. Plucking the head is too laborious, so skinning the skull is the better option for those wishing to follow this culinary practice.

1 Pluck away a few of the feathers at the base of the skull on the back of the bird's head to create a bald patch of skin.

2 Remove the skin from the head by pinching the bald patch and pulling it over the head towards the beak. Pick off any stray pieces of skin or feathers.

Tips for Cooking Woodcock

• If the innards seem a little inadequate, help them go further by adding a little pâté or terrine *de fois gras* before spreading them on toast or fried bread.

• The widespread notion that the tendons running the length of the woodcock's legs can taint the flesh and should be removed before cooking is completely untrue.

• To prevent the brain drying out during cooking, the skinned head can be wrapped in a small piece of foil during roasting.

• Woodcock were often blamed for causing indigestion and stomach upsets, but this may have been a consequence of hanging them for up to a fortnight: one or two days, somewhere dark and cold, is quite sufficient for an undamaged bird.

1 First remove the gizzard, which is tough and contains grit and other unpalatable matter. With the bird on its back, make a small cut between the first rib and the thigh on the bird's right flank.

2 With a slim curved skewer or similar instrument, locate the gizzard and hook it out through the small incision you've made in the bird's side.

3 The gizzard is easily recognized as the small ribbed muscular organ, about 1cm (½ in) in length. It feels firm and slightly rubbery. Cut through the connecting tissue and discard the gizzard.

4 Push a thin skewer through one thigh, through the bird's stomach area and then out through the other thigh.

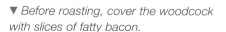
▼ *Before roasting, cover the woodcock with slices of fatty bacon.*

5 Keeping the beak as tightly closed as possible, guide it into the hole you have just made with the skewer. The beak will naturally open a little once it is pushed all the way through, which will secure its position and keep it in place.

6 Cross the bird's legs and knot with a single loop of butcher's string. The woodcock is now ready to be cooked.

▼ *Instead of roasting, discard the head and innards, and fry, basting frequently.*

Preparing and Trussing Snipe

This tiny little bird offers no more than a morsel of joy and is really best roasted for around 10–13 minutes, undrawn with the gizzard removed, and with a little fatty bacon secured over its tender breast. Like the woodcock, the head can be left on or removed. Grilling (broiling) the birds for 8–10 minutes also gives them the intense heat they need, but with a little more control.

Traditionally, after roasting, snipe are served on a small piece of toasted or fried bread that has been smeared with the mashed innards and drizzled with a little brandy and game fumet – a highly concentrated game stock.

If you have an accomplished team that has managed to shoot snipe in significant numbers, then a slightly more modern approach is to 'fly them through the oven', smeared in olive oil and with a good twist of white pepper. Serve them on the pink side, four or five each, accompanied by root vegetable chips and a very dusty bottle from the northern Rhone – Côte-Rôtie or Crozes-Hermitage perhaps.

▲ *If the bird has been feeding in the waters of an estuary rather than inland waters, a snipe's meat can sometimes harbour a slight trace of the coastline in its flavour.*

Skinning a Snipe's Head

As with the woodcock, preparing the snipe's head by skinning it is much less labour-intensive than plucking all the tiny feathers.

Pluck a few feathers at the base of the skull, then remove the skin by pinching the bald patch and pulling it over the head towards the beak.

REMOVING THE GIZZARD FROM SNIPE

1 As with the woodcock, the snipe's gizzard should always be removed; it contains grit and other unpalatable matter that could spoil the innards and the highly flavoured juices. With the bird on its back, make a shallow cut with the tip of a sharp knife between the first rib and the thigh on the bird's right flank.

2 With a slim curved skewer or similar instrument, locate the gizzard and hook it out through the incision you've made. With your knife, cut through the connecting tissue and throw away the gizzard. Even if you managed to thoroughly clean out this organ, cooking does nothing other than turn it solid, rubbery and inedible.

TRUSSING SNIPE WITH ITS BEAK

1 To truss a snipe using its beak, punch a very thin skewer through one of its thighs, then through the stomach and out through the other thigh.

2 Keeping the beak as tightly closed as possible with your fingers, guide the closed beak into the hole you've just made with the skewer.

3 Once the beak is pushed all the way through, it will naturally open a little, securing its position.

4 To finish, cross the bird's legs and knot with a loop or two of butcher's string, trimming away any excess.

5 If you are going to flash-roast the snipe, lard it with some fatty bacon or pancetta to keep the flesh moist.

Tips for Cooking Snipe

• An old Italian method for keeping *uccelletti* (small birds of any kind) moist during cooking is to roast them in a fierce oven with each bird nestled into the cap of a large mushroom or even half a small potato, hollowed out. The vegetable protects the bird from direct contact with the pan. You'll need to experiment with timings.

• There is little value in hanging snipe; it's best to get them prepared and eaten as quickly as possible.

• If you're lucky enough to be serving a good number of snipe to your closest friends, don't bother with cutlery – just provide big napkins and finger bowls. Eating small game birds with your fingers ensures that nothing is wasted and you glean every delicious scrap.

• The traditional Christmas accompaniment of Brussels sprouts with either chopped chestnuts and smoky bacon or pancetta lardons makes a great side dish for snipe.

• Most traditional recipes suggest adding brandy to snipe dishes, but Madeira also lends itself well.

◀ *Traditionally, snipe are placed on fried bread, on to which the entrails have been spread, and served with oysters.*

Preparing Grouse

Their diet of young heather shoots, seeds and berries gives grouse a completely unique flavour but, it has to be said, they can be a little too strong for some people. In very cold weather, hanging for three days is plenty, and in mild weather they'll need to be drawn within the day unless you like them green and rather bitter. It isn't that unusual for a shooting party to take a portable barbecue out with them and cook any shot birds straight away. As the coals are heating up, the party will sit among the heather plucking and drawing the bag.

If you wish to roast grouse simply, the birds must be young. Without question, older birds should be cooked slowly. Slow braising in gutsy red wine works beautifully, as do sauces made with berries. When inspecting the birds in the feather, concentrate on the outer primary feathers. These should be sharp and pointed, with the third one slightly shorter sometimes. Blunt, rounded feathers of similar length suggest an older bird that should not be roasted.

▶ *The slightest over-hanging of these birds can result in their ruination.*

▼ *The flavour of the dark, rich, red meat from a red grouse is one of the strongest and gamiest.*

1 Score the skin between the claw and the knuckle. Holding the joint tightly in one hand, twist the claw and draw out all the tendons from the thigh.

2 Holding the bird breast down, run the point of the knife up the centre of the neck and away from you.

3 Holding the neck skin and the crop in one hand, pull the neck away from the crop and skin. Wrapping the neck stump in a little kitchen paper can help you grip the skinned neck. Be careful not to tear the membrane of the crop.

4 Cut through the neck stump and remove it. Carefully separate the windpipe from the skin of the neck. Stretching the windpipe and gullet leading to the crop, cut through this close to the bird's body

5 Push a finger into the cavity where the neck was and twist it around to release the tissues securing the organs. Be cautious if you think the ribs have been broken by shot, as you may stab your finger on splintered bones.

6 Turning the bird on to its back, pinch the skin at the tip of the breastbone, just above the vent, and cut down halfway, (but not all the way through) to expose the entrails.

7 Carefully cut around the vent, leaving this intact.

▶ *Try to keep the grouse looking tidy as you prepare it, and take your time.*

8 Push one or two fingers into the cavity and remove the contents in one motion.

Tips for Cooking Grouse

• For a slight twist on a traditional accompaniment, instead of serving the standard potato game chips with grouse, try using parsnips, cut wafer-thin with a mandolin and deep-fried.
• Avoid marinades containing wine, as grouse tend to take on an almost pickled flavour when it is used. The most effective marinade ingredients for grouse are sliced onions, celery, carrots, olive oil, a little lemon juice and crushed juniper berries.

• A young grouse, halved, liberally brushed with butter and well seasoned, will grill very well indeed; 5 minutes on each side is plenty.
• If you like your meat rare to the point of bloody, preheat the oven to its highest setting and quickly colour the birds in a pan, just enough to brown the skin, then roast them in the hot oven for just 7 minutes. Leave them to rest in a warm place for a good 20–30 minutes before serving.

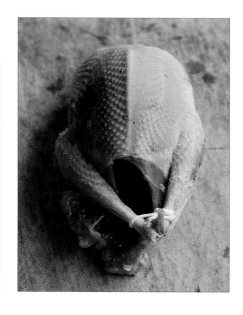

Preparing and Spatchcocking Quail

The only real difference between farmed and wild varieties of quail is that the farmed birds hold a little more natural fat, which helps keep them moist during cooking. The birds that are shot, however, do have an edge when it comes to natural flavour.

Because of its size, quail is the perfect bird to cook quickly outdoors, on a spit in the field or on a barbecue. One idea that works very well is to tumble some ripe tomatoes into a shallow roasting pan together with some olive oil and fresh herbs – such as rosemary, basil and thyme – and leave them on the barbecue to cook down and burst in the pan as your quail cooks over the coals. Warm some ciabatta bread, strip the meat from the birds on to it, drizzle with the tomato mixture and add a little blue cheese for a truly stunning open sandwich.

If you want something a little more filling, many risotto recipes benefit from the addition of grilled quail; you can even make some shellfish risotto dishes a little more hearty by stirring some shredded quail through them.

▶ *The quail that make their way most regularly to the table are the Bobwhite and Japanese strains.*

1 Score the skin between the claw and the bird's knee joint. With the knuckle tightly gripped in one hand, twist the claw slowly, drawing out the tendons from the leg. (This will ensure that the leg will not dry out during cooking.)

2 Holding the bird breast down, run the knife up the centre of the neck and away from you. Holding the neck skin and the crop in the left hand, pull the neck away from the crop and skin. Cut through the neck stump and remove it.

3 Carefully separate the windpipe from the skin of the neck. Stretching the windpipe and the gullet, which leads to the crop, cut through this close to the bird's body.

4 Turn the bird on to its back and pinch the skin at the tip of the breastbone, just above the vent. Cut down lightly through the skin, exposing the entrails. Make a circular cut around the vent, leaving this area intact.

5 Push a finger into the cavity where the neck was. Rotating your finger around inside will release the fibres connecting the organs to the bird. Push one or two fingers into the cavity and remove the contents in one motion.

6 Wipe the bird's cavity thoroughly with kitchen paper, then pat the bird dry, inside and out. The kidneys, either side of the backbone, can stay inside: they are too small to remove and will add a little flavour.

SPATCHCOCKING QUAIL

1 With a knife or a pair of game or poultry shears, cut down along one side of the bird's backbone, starting at the cavity end. Repeat this process on the other side and remove the spine.

2 Lay the bird down on a board with the breast uppermost, and press down hard on the breast with the palm of your hand to flatten the bird out.

3 The bird is now spatchcocked and ready for cooking.

▼ *Insert metal skewers to help distribute the heat if you wish.*

Tips for Cooking Quail
• Barbecue or grill (broil) a spatchcocked quail, coated in plain yogurt mixed with ground cumin, cardamom, fenugreek and coriander. Add some turmeric for colour, and a little chilli for heat.
• Spatchcocked quail can also be slathered in good olive oil and very well seasoned with freshly milled black pepper and the finest sea salt, celery salt or even garlic salt.

Colour the birds well in a pan then roast in a hot oven for 20 minutes.
• For a bird that's completely at home on the plantations, what better side dish than creamed corn?
• Try lightly smoking quail to boost their mild flavour. They don't need long at all. Experiment with different wood smoke and try adding a small scoop of fragrant tea leaves to the wood: Earl Grey works well.

Preparing and Trussing Guinea Fowl

Although the guinea fowl is strictly a poultry bird, it has the unusual status of often being included with game when considered for the table. Of course, these curious birds are indeed shot in many countries, particularly in Africa, but in many others you could be fined for shooting one.

Unlike almost every other game bird, the guinea fowl manages to maintain a generous layer of fat that keeps its flesh wonderfully moist and succulent during cooking. Unlike most chicken, however, it has an almost guaranteed degree of flavour regardless of its diet.

If you are buying guinea fowl from a butcher the birds will have been despatched at an age judged just right for the table, but if you've shot the birds yourself, you'll cope with whatever you've harvested. For older birds, opt for a slow cooking recipe to ensure a really succulent meal without any surprising disappointments.

▶ *Chicken, partridge and pheasant recipes all work well with these incredibly tasty birds.*

1 Starting at the feet, cut the skin between the claw and the knuckle. Grip the knuckle in one hand, twist the claw and draw out the tendons from the leg.

2 Hold the bird breast down and run the knife up the centre of the neck, away from you.

3 Hold the neck skin and the crop (the thin membrane holding undigested food matter) in your left hand, and pull the neck away from the crop. Cut through the neck stump, twist and remove.

4 Separate the windpipe from the skin of the neck. Cut the windpipe and gullet. Push your finger into the cavity and twist it round to release the tissues connecting the organs.

5 Turn the bird on to its back, pinch the skin at the tip of the breastbone, above the vent, and cut down halfway, to expose the entrails. Cut round the vent.

6 Push one or two fingers into the cavity and remove the contents in one motion. Wipe the bird's cavity thoroughly with kitchen paper.

7 If you suspect the gut may have been torn by shot, rinse the bird's cavity under cold running water, then pat the bird dry, inside and out.

TRUSSING GUINEA FOWL

If you are roasting a bird it is a good idea to truss it. This technique – tying the legs and wings so that they remain close to the body – means that the bird will cook more evenly and is less likely to dry out. The following instructions can be used for trussing any size of bird. You will need to use 100 per cent cotton butcher's string.

1 Cut a length of butcher's string about 60cm/24in long. With the bird breast up, pass the string under the legs.

2 Knot the string in the middle, on top of the legs.

3 Pull tight and then pass the two ends between the legs and the tail (or 'parson's nose'). Pull the ends taut.

4 Turn the bird over on to its breast, looping the string ends over too.

5 Pass each end of the string under and past the corresponding leg, finishing under each wing.

6 Place the flap of skin from the neck between the wings and knot it twice to secure. Cut off the surplus string. The trussed bird is now ready for roasting.

Tips for Cooking Guinea Fowl

• Unlike game birds, these birds manage to retain a little extra fat, which will help you when pan-frying the breast. The extra 'cushion' provided by the fat can also allow you to be a little more adventurous without fear of the meat drying out.

• Old and largely forgotten recipes for poached chicken work even better with guinea fowl, as they maintain the flavour that most modern chickens lack.

• As with chicken, tarragon works beautifully as a flavouring for guinea fowl, as does chervil.

Salad of Hot-smoked Teal

The small breasts of the teal are ideal for this quick hot-smoking method. Instead of wood chips, a mixture of rice, sugar and aromatic Earl Grey tea is used to give a smoky flavour. You will need a small gas stove or open fire to cook this recipe. The pickled figs can be prepared at home in advance.

Serves 2

4 teal breasts
15ml/1tbsp vegetable oil
175g/6oz/¾ cup long grain rice
110g/4oz/½ cup demerara (raw) sugar
25g/1oz Earl Grey tea
1 fat head radicchio or travissio leaves, roughly chopped
115g/4oz fine green beans, blanched in salted boiling water for 2 minutes
sea salt and ground black pepper

For the pickled figs
450g/1lb dried figs
225g/8oz/1 generous cup sugar
275ml/10fl oz red wine vinegar

For the dressing
25g/1oz pecan nuts, toasted and chopped
45ml/3 tbsp extra virgin olive oil
15ml/1 tbsp red wine vinegar
sea salt and ground black pepper

1 To make the pickled figs, put the figs, sugar and vinegar into a pan with 275ml/9fl oz water and bring to the boil, stirring, to dissolve the sugar. Cook for 1 minute, then reduce the heat and simmer very gently for approximately 10 minutes, until the figs appear plump.

Cook's tip To make this into a main course, add one extra breast per person and toss some croûtons or cooked potatoes through the salad.

2 Spoon the figs into a sterilized jar with a tight-fitting lid, cover with the syrup and leave to cool. There will be more figs than you need for the salad.

3 Make a trivet by folding three layers of foil into a rough circle the size of the pan and scrunching it into waves.

4 Place a frying pan over high heat. Season the teal breasts with salt and pepper. Add the oil to the pan and leave it to get very hot before laying the breasts in the pan and sealing them very quickly and briefly on all sides. Remove.

5 Make the salad dressing by placing all the ingredients in a jar with a tight-fitting lid and shaking to amalgamate.

6 Mix the rice, sugar and tea in a shallow pan and warm it over low heat until the mixture begins to smoke.

7 Lay the foil trivet in the pan, place the teal breasts on top and seal with more foil and the pan lid. Cook over low heat for 6 minutes, then remove from the heat and allow to cool, still sealed.

8 Remove the teal breasts from the pan and slice thinly crossways. Divide the salad leaves between two bowls and arrange the beans, teal and figs over them. Dress with a little of the fig liquor, the dressing and some seasoning.

Energy 526kcal/2189kJ; Protein 26.1g; Carbohydrate 27.8g, of which sugars 27g; Fat 35.3g, of which saturates 4.7g; Cholesterol 43mg; Calcium 168mg; Fibre 5.8g; Sodium 102mg

Camp-Fire Woodland Pigeon

Wood pigeon is one of the most accessible game birds available. As you can be pretty confident of bagging one this dish is ideal for cooking in the field. Fried potatoes and eggs are one of the culinary world's finest yet simplest of marriages, and they create a great base on which to build this dish.

Serves 1

275g/10oz potatoes
2 pigeon breasts
15ml/1 tbsp olive oil
75g/3oz cooking chorizo,
    thickly sliced
1 egg
10ml/2 tsp capers in brine, drained
sea salt and ground black pepper

3 Heat a frying pan, add the oil and wait for it to get hot before putting the breasts in, skin down. Cook for 1½ minutes, then turn and cook for another 1½ minutes. Remove from the pan.

6 Push the potato and chorizo mixture to one side of the pan. Making sure the oil is still hot, break the egg into the empty side of the pan and fry.

1 Bring a pan of salted water to the boil, add the potatoes and return to a simmer. When they are almost cooked, drain and leave to cool slightly.

2 When the potatoes are cool enough to handle, cut into 1cm/½in cubes and season with salt and pepper. Season the pigeon with salt and pepper.

4 Add the potatoes to the pan and cook, turning occasionally, until golden and crisp. Add the chorizo and fry for 3–5 minutes, stirring to coat the potatoes in the spicy juices.

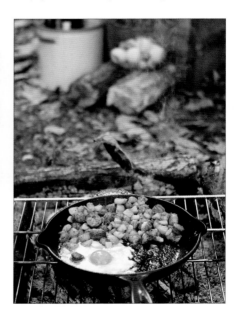

7 When the egg is cooked to your liking, add the pigeon slices to the potato, sprinkle with the capers and fold through the potato mixture.

8 Transfer the potatoes and pigeon to a plate and top with the egg, or eat straight from the pan.

5 Meanwhile, while the chorizo and potato mixture cooks, use a sharp knife to slice the pigeon breasts, widthways. Cover and set aside.

Variations Hare loin, venison loin, duck breasts or partridge breasts are all good substitutes for the pigeon. If you don't like capers, add 10ml/2 tsp sherry vinegar instead to cut the richness.

Energy 762kcal/3184kJ; Protein 39g; Carbohydrate 53g, of which sugars 4.9g; Fat 45.3g, of which saturates 10.9g; Cholesterol 220mg; Calcium 93mg; Fibre 3.1g; Sodium 790mg

Snipe with Stout and Oysters

Usually inhabiting marshy uplands, snipe can also occasionally be found wading in salt marshes.
If you are hunting in these coastal areas, a marriage of snipe and oysters found in the salty inlets makes
for a luxurious, protein-rich meal that can easily be cooked over an open fire or on a portable stove.
You will need a pan with a tight-fitting lid to cook the birds, plus a frying pan.

Serves 2

2 snipe, cleaned (reserve the livers and
  hearts for another dish)
115g/4oz/½ cup duck fat or butter
1 large onion, finely diced
3 garlic cloves, sliced
275ml/9floz/generous 1 cup stout
2 thick slices soda bread
6 oysters
15ml/1 tbsp chopped parsley
sea salt and ground black pepper

1 Season the snipe with salt and
pepper. Heat a pan over the fire and
add 50g/2oz of the fat.

2 When the fat is sizzling, place the
snipe in the pan, turning to brown on
all sides, then remove and reserve.

3 Add the onions to the pan and cook
gently for 8–10 minutes, stirring
occasionally. When the onions are soft
add one-third of the sliced garlic.

4 When the garlic has released its
aroma, return the snipe to the pan.

5 Add the stout to the pan, cover tightly
and braise gently for 20 minutes on the
edge of the fire.

6 Heat a frying pan on the fire and add
the remaining fat. Add the garlic and
cook for 1 minute. Place the two slices
of bread in the pan and fry until golden
on both sides.

7 To finish, open the oysters and add
the flesh and any liquor to the pan.

8 Add the parsley, check the seasoning,
replace the lid and remove from the
heat. Serve the snipe and oysters on
the fried bread.

Variation If it is difficult to get hold of
(or transport) fresh oysters, use tinned
or frozen ones, together with 15ml/
1 tbsp oyster sauce for extra flavour.

Energy 688kcal/2868kJ; Protein 37.9g; Carbohydrate 39.5g, of which sugars 9.3g; Fat 39.7g, of which saturates 20.4g; Cholesterol 129mg; Calcium 253mg; Fibre 2.9g; Sodium 963mg

Fireside Snipe with Bread Sauce and Ham Stovey

Snipe is traditionally cooked with its entrails intact. After cooking, the guts can be drawn and either spread on toast or used to fortify the gravy, as here. The snipe is a fairly small bird and not always easy to come by; serving the birds with potato cake and bread sauce helps them go further.

Serves 4

4 snipe, gizzards removed
115g/4oz/½ cup butter
250ml/8fl oz/1 cup ruby port
sea salt and ground black pepper

For the bread sauce
275ml/9fl oz/generous 1 cup full-fat
   (whole) milk
1 small onion, sliced
4 cloves
freshly grated nutmeg
1 bay leaf
50g/2oz/1 cup soft white breadcrumbs
50g/2oz/¼ cup butter
sea salt and ground black pepper

For the ham stovey
50g/2oz/¼ cup butter
1 large onion, sliced
350g/12oz cooked smoked ham, diced
675g/1½lb cooked potato, mashed
10ml/2 tsp English (hot)
   mustard powder
30ml/2 tbsp fresh parsley, chopped

1 To make the bread sauce, put the milk, onion, cloves, nutmeg and bay leaf in a small pan and heat gently to a simmer. Turn off the heat, cover the pan and leave to infuse (steep) for 1 hour.

2 Truss each snipe by pushing its beak through one drumstick into the other, over the breastbone, making incisions with a knife to help you. Season the birds well with salt and pepper.

3 Heat the butter in a pan. Place the snipe in the pan on their sides and seal, repeat on the other side, then lay the birds on their backs. Cook for 12 minutes, basting regularly with the butter. When cooked, remove from the pan and leave to rest.

4 Meanwhile make the ham stovey. Heat a frying pan over medium heat and add the butter. Add the onion and cook, stirring, for 5–8 minutes until softened.

5 Add the ham to the pan and heat thoroughly before adding the mashed potato, mustard powder, parsley and seasoning. Mix with a wooden spoon and spread the mixture out in the pan.

6 Fry the stovey on one side until golden, then turn it over to cook the other side. When cooked, set the pan on the edge of the fire to keep warm.

Variation Try adding cooked, chopped Brussels sprouts or Savoy cabbage to the stovey.

7 To finish the bread sauce, add the breadcrumbs to the milk and heat gently for approximately 5 minutes, stirring, until smooth and thickened. Add the butter and plenty of salt and pepper.

8 Transfer the birds to a plate and draw the guts by slitting the skin across the rear end and scooping out the contents with a spoon. Separate out the livers and discard the rest of the entrails.

9 Break up the livers with a fork and add to the pan in which the snipe were cooked. Add the port, boil for 2 minutes and finish by adding any juices that have drained from the birds.

10 Serve the snipe with a drizzle of port and liver sauce, a generous spoonful of bread sauce, and a slice of stovey.

Energy 891kcal/3714kJ; Protein 41.3g; Carbohydrate 52.8g, of which sugars 17.3g; Fat 50.6g, of which saturates 26.5g; Cholesterol 161mg; Calcium 170mg; Fibre 3.3g; Sodium 1598mg

Barbecue Grouse with Roasted Vegetables

Preparing a bird by spatchcocking is ideal for cooking outside on a wood fire or barbecue, as it creates a uniform thickness of meat for more even cooking. The grouse will benefit from marinating before cooking: lemon is used here to give a fresh, zingy flavour.

Serves 2

30ml/2 tbsp olive oil
juice of 2 lemons
4 garlic cloves, finely grated
6 thyme sprigs, rubbed to release
   the flavour
2 grouse, drawn and cleaned
1 courgette (zucchini), sliced
   diagonally
1 red (bell) pepper, cut into wide strips
1 aubergine (eggplant), cut into rounds
sea salt and ground black pepper
bread, to serve

1 Mix the oil, lemon juice, garlic, thyme and seasoning in a bowl. Pour half the marinade into a flat dish.

2 To spatchcock the grouse, hold each bird with the backbone upwards. Cut along either side of the backbone with scissors or poultry shears to remove it.

3 Turn the grouse over and place it on a chopping board. Open out the ribcage, pushing down firmly to flatten it.

4 Add the grouse to the marinade in the large dish, rubbing it into the meat, and set aside for at least 20 minutes.

Variation You could use quail instead of grouse in this recipe.

5 When you have glowing embers on your fire or barbecue, place the courgette, red pepper and aubergine slices on the grill rack and cook for 5–6 minutes on each side until browned. As the vegetables are done, remove them from the grill and mix into the reserved marinade. Set aside.

6 Brush the marinade off the grouse and place the birds skin side down on the barbecue. Cook for 5–6 minutes then turn and cook for another 5–6 minutes.

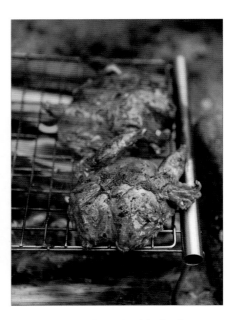

7 Turn back to the skin side for 2 more minutes, flip again for 2 minutes then move the grouse to the edge of the fire to rest. Serve with the roasted vegetable salad and some fresh bread.

Energy 559kcal/2342kJ; Protein 75.7g; Carbohydrate 9.6g, of which sugars 9.1g; Fat 24.4g, of which saturates 4.7g; Cholesterol 0mg; Calcium 112mg; Fibre 4.3g; Sodium 227mg

One-pot Quail and Sauerkraut

Being a small bird, quail can dry out quickly, so this braising method is a perfect way of cooking it, and the fruity, sweet wine in which it is cooked in this recipe is a great complement to its delicate flavour. This recipe is ideal for cooking outside, as it is all cooked in one big pot hung over the fire.

Serves 2

50g/2oz/4 tbsp lard
50g/2oz smoked streaky (fatty) bacon, cut into narrow strips
1 large onion, finely sliced
4 quail, dressed and drawn
1 large carrot, peeled and thinly sliced
6 juniper berries, lightly crushed
leaves from 2 thyme sprigs
300ml/½ pint/1¼ cups Riesling or similar German wine
300g/11oz jar sauerkraut
150g/5oz Bavarian smoked sausage, sliced 5mm/¼in thick
500g/1¼lb floury potatoes, peeled and cubed
50g/2oz/4 tbsp butter
45ml/3 tbsp milk
sea salt and ground black pepper

Cook's tip If you have no Bavarian sausage, try cooked smoked ham.

Variation Squirrel would also work well if cooked in this way – extend the cooking time to 1½–2 hours before adding the sauerkraut and sausage.

1 Warm the pot. Add the lard, and when melted, add the bacon and onions and fry, stirring, until the onions are softened.

2 Add the quail and carrot, season with plenty of salt and pepper and cook for 5 minutes to colour the birds.

3 Add the juniper berries, thyme and wine to the pot with 300ml/½ pint/1¼ cups water; cook gently for 30 minutes.

4 When the quail is just tender, add the sauerkraut and sausage, replace the lid and cook for another 10–15 minutes, or until the contents are thoroughly hot.

5 Meanwhile, place the potatoes in a pan and cover with water, adding a good pinch of salt. Bring to the boil and simmer for 15 minutes until tender. Drain, return to the pan and add the butter, milk and some seasoning. Mash until smooth and serve with the quail.

Energy 1276kcal/5307kJ; Protein 48.6g; Carbohydrate 60.6g, of which sugars 13.9g; Fat 84.4g, of which saturates 33.7g; Cholesterol 128mg; Calcium 214mg; Fibre 7.6g; Sodium 2155mg

Fire-grilled Quail with Punched Potatoes

The Portuguese love cooking simple, unfussy food outside. This dish is a prime example: the quail (or codorniz as they are known) are quickly grilled over a hot wood fire and eaten with potatoes that have been cooked in the embers and 'punched' before serving to make them light and fluffy.

Serves 1

3–4 thyme sprigs
45ml/3 tbsp extra virgin olive oil
2 garlic cloves, crushed
1 lemon
2 quail
2 red-skinned potatoes, scrubbed
sea salt and ground black pepper
butter and Little Gem (Bibb) lettuce,
    to serve

1 To make the marinade, strip the leaves from the thyme sprigs and place them in a screw-top jar with the oil and garlic. Grate the lemon rind into the jar, reserving the lemon. Screw on the lid and shake to emulsify.

2 To spatchcock the quail, take each bird in one hand, backbone facing upwards, and with a pair of scissors or poultry shears cut along either side of the backbone to remove it. Place the quail breast up on a chopping board and open out the ribcage, pushing down firmly to flatten it.

3 Put the quail into a plastic bag, add the marinade and massage into the birds through the bag. Seal the bag and leave to marinate for 45 minutes.

4 Using a double thickness of foil, wrap the potatoes individually, adding a little salt and pepper before you seal them. Place in the fire at the side where the heat isn't too intense.

5 Cover the potatoes with a few glowing embers and cook for about 1 hour, turning every 15 minutes or so. Test by inserting a knife into the largest. When soft, keep warm at the side of the fire.

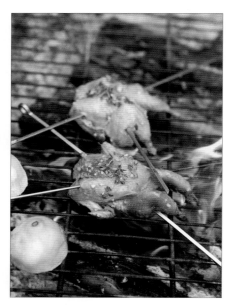

6 Season the quail and lay them on a grill rack, or arrange on skewers above the fire. Grill for around 10–15 minutes, turning the birds every few minutes to ensure even cooking.

7 'Punch' the potatoes so the skins split and the steam escapes, giving a fluffy texture. Add a knob of butter and drizzle over a little juice from the reserved lemon. Once the quail are cooked, squeeze the remaining lemon juice over. Serve with potatoes and lettuce leaves.

Energy 679kcal/2828kJ; Protein 32.7g; Carbohydrate 32.2g, of which sugars 2.6g; Fat 47.5g, of which saturates 4.8g; Cholesterol 0mg; Calcium 29mg; Fibre 2g; Sodium 132mg

Guinea Fowl Cacciatore

Cacciatore means 'in the style of the hunter' and so is ideal for cooking outside. The recipe can be used for most game meat, although the light-coloured game bird meats such as pheasant, turkey or in this case guinea fowl are more commonly used. This is a simple one-pan dish that can easily be cooked on a fire or portable stove, and requires no more than some pasta to accompany it.

Serves 4

60ml/4 tbsp olive oil
1 medium onion, thinly sliced
1 green (bell) pepper, sliced
1 red (bell) pepper, sliced
4 garlic cloves, peeled and sliced
1 guinea fowl, boned and cut into
   finger-sized strips
12 brown cap (cremini) mushrooms,
   halved
150ml/¼ pint/⅔ cup white wine
500g/1¼lb jar tomato pasta sauce
15–20 black olives, pitted
15ml/1 tbsp chopped oregano
15ml/1 tbsp chopped basil
300g/11oz long pasta (spaghetti,
   linguine or tagliatelle)
sea salt and ground black pepper

1 Put a wide casserole over medium heat; add 45ml/3 tbsp of olive oil and the sliced onion and cook, stirring, for 5 minutes.

2 Add the peppers and garlic to the onions and fry quickly for 2 minutes.

3 Add the strips of guinea fowl to the onion and peppers. Season well and cook for 4–5 minutes until the meat is coloured. Add the mushrooms and cook for a further 5 minutes.

4 Add the wine to the pan, bring to the boil and then add the pasta sauce. Bring the liquid back to the boil, then move the pan to a less intense part of the fire so that it simmers gently.

5 Cook the sauce for 20 minutes, stirring occasionally.

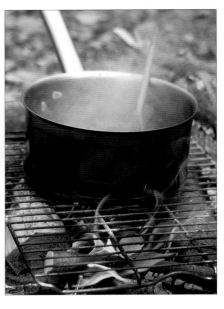

6 Add the olives and the herbs, reserving a handful to garnish. Adjust the seasoning and keep warm while you cook the pasta.

7 Bring a large pan of salted water to the boil, add the pasta, bring back to the boil and stir. Continue to boil vigorously for 9–11 minutes or until the pasta is al dente.

8 Drain the pasta then return it to the pan. Season to taste, toss in the remaining olive oil, sprinkle with the reserved herbs and serve with the cooked guinea fowl.

Energy 718kcal/3021kJ; Protein 52.1g; Carbohydrate 66.4g, of which sugars 12.6g; Fat 26.4g, of which saturates 6.1g; Cholesterol 0mg; Calcium 113mg; Fibre 5.6g; Sodium 433mg

LARGE FEATHERED GAME

Whether you've just taken your first turkey of the season, or a brace of pheasant on your last syndicate day, the following pages offer various recipes, hints and suggestions to help you get the most from your birds. Everyone has a favourite way of cooking their most frequently obtained quarry, but if you have a particularly good day, with a glut of birds, your priority will be to pluck and draw a large number as efficiently as possible and convert them all into a meal in some way. A roasted bird with all the traditional accompaniments makes a wonderful meal, but sometimes there is only time to whip out the breast fillets and legs and freeze them for use at a later date in a braise or a spiced sauce. Responsible usage is paramount, whether you have a single bird to take home or several.

◀ *Larger game birds, such as partridge and pheasant, need to be slowly braised for the tenderest result. Their delicious flavour works well with robust ingredients, as in this pheasant casserole with red wine and prunes.*

Plucking a Large Bird

While it is easy to pluck a small bird between your legs, with no tools other than your hands, with a larger bird such as a turkey or a goose you may find it easier to hang it. For this you will need a butcher's hook or some strong, thick string that will not stretch, use this to tie the feet together, leaving a loop of string to loop on to a hook or beam. Hang the bird so that its feet are at about your eye level and its body is hanging at a comfortable height for you.

▶ *Turkey feathers, like those of most other large birds, are large and fairly easy to remove. There is less chance of the skin tearing than with small birds.*

1 When you have hung the bird, begin by pulling one wing out and pluck it from the inside outwards.

2 Now run the knife along the quill part of the feather, where it meets the retaining skin.

3 Once under the edge of these leading feathers, run the knife along the length of this 'rail' of bone.

4 The thin but tough piece of skin securing all the feathers will come away in one piece.

5 Repeat the process with the other wing. You can do this on a board before hanging if you find it easier.

6 Now begin plucking the bird's back. Although turkey feathers are much bigger than those of a small bird, you still need to pluck just a few at a time.

7 When the back is clear, move on to the turkey's legs. Pull each one towards you as you pluck.

8 Once the legs are completely plucked, you can begin work on the breast area, one side at a time.

9 When you have done both sides of the breast, pluck as far up the neck as possible, almost to the head.

10 Last of all, concentrate on the rather tricky long tail feathers. Then take the bird down and finish it on a board.

11 Clear the neck of any feathers. Remove the wiry brush at the top of the breast and discard. Remove the head with a machete or a heavy knife. The bird is now reading for drawing.

▲ *A turkey and cranberry pie made with filleted-out breast meat is an impressive alternative to a whole roasted bird.*

Preparing and Spatchcocking Partridge

The partridge is the ideal beginner's game bird, as it offers a wonderfully subtle whiff of gaminess without being too strong or overbearing.

These days it's unusual to end up with a partridge that is too old to do anything with. However, if you must have a young grey partridge, look for very pale legs and a beak that has yet to darken to a flinty grey colour. A first-season red-legged or French partridge should ideally have a yielding, pliable breastbone. As both of these wonderful little birds are prone to dryness, braising, pot-roasting and careful roasting are the methods that produce the most satisfying results.

Traditional recipes tend to favour earthy complementary flavours, with ingredients such as kale, cabbage and lentils. All these serve the partridge beautifully, but as it can be bought and shot easily, let your imagination run riot with anything from a Cajun-spiced rub before roasting to spatchcocking and grilling, slathered in butter and honey.

▶ *Partridge needs no more than two or three days' hanging at the most, in a cold place such as a chilly outbuilding.*

1 First remove the feet. Cut the skin between the claw and the knuckle or 'knee' joint to minimize shrinkage and drying during cooking. Grip the knuckle tightly and twist the claw slowly, drawing out the tendons from the leg.

2 Discard the claw and tendons. Now, holding the bird breast down, make a cut through the skin by running the knife up the centre of the neck and away from you.

3 Holding the neck skin and the crop in one hand, pull the neck away from the crop and skin with the other. Cut through the neck stump, twist and remove it. Separate the windpipe from the skin of the neck. Stretching the windpipe and gullet (which leads to the crop), cut through this close to the body.

4 Push a finger into the cavity and twist it round to release the tissues connecting the organs to the bird.

5 Turn the bird on to its back, pinch the skin at the tip of the breastbone, just above the vent, and cut down halfway.

6 Cut carefully right round the vent, leaving this intact.

7 Push one or two fingers into the cavity and remove the contents in one motion The kidneys will still be inside the bird.

8 Wipe the cavity thoroughly with some kitchen paper. Afterwards, pat the bird dry, inside and out.

Roast Partridge with Stuffing

For two people you need a bird each. Preheat the oven to 200°C/400°F/Gas 6. Prepare the partridges, then stuff them with a mixture of black pudding and white pudding (boudin blanc). Do not overfill the cavity as the stuffing will expand during cooking; around two-thirds full should be fine. Oil the skin lightly, season, then roast in the hot oven for 20–30 minutes, until golden and cooked through. Remove from the oven and allow to stand then serve with bread sauce, game chips and some wilted greens.

SPATCHCOCKING PARTRIDGE

1 First remove the parson's nose. Using poultry shears, cut along both sides of the bird's backbone, starting at the cavity end, and remove the bone.

2 Alternatively, you can fold the bird back on itself, skin-to-skin, and snip out the spine this way.

3 Lay the bird down on a board, with the breast uppermost, and press down hard on the breast to flatten it out.

Preparing and Quartering Duck

The duck offers a wealth of culinary opportunities for keen shots across the world. An adult mallard is large enough to feed two people, and is rarely difficult to find. The hardest thing to ascertain is what it has been feeding on. If your duck has been eating good quality grain or root tops you will enjoy a tasty meal. However, if it has been scavenging around muddy estuaries, then it will taste of just that.

Although many recipes for farmed duck work with wild birds, the latter do not possess anything like as much fat, so you will need to add extra.

▶ *The mallard is universally shot by shooters seeking wildfowl.*

1 Start with the feet. With a sharp knife or a blow from a cleaver, remove the foot around halfway up the shin bone.

2 With the bird breast-down, run the knife up the back of the neck and away from you. Remove and discard the head.

3 Holding the neck skin and the crop in one hand, pull the neck away from the crop and skin with the other.

4 Cut through the neck stump and remove it. Carefully separate the windpipe from the skin of the neck.

5 Stretching the windpipe and gullet, which extends to the crop, sever this close to the duck's body. Be careful not to tear the crop membrane.

6 Push a finger through and into the cavity where the neck was and twist it round to release the tissues connecting the organs to the body.

7 Turn the duck on to its back, pinch the skin at the tip of the breastbone, just above the vent, and cut down halfway. Cut a circle round the vent.

8 Push two fingers into the cavity and withdraw the contents in one swift motion. The kidneys can be left in place.

9 Wipe the cavity with kitchen paper. Rinse with cold running water if you suspect the gut has been punctured.

Tips for Cooking Wild Duck
- If the webbing on the duck's feet is easily torn, it indicates a young bird suitable for roasting. A springy breastbone is another sign.
- If you suspect that a duck may taste a little muddy, soak it overnight in a mixture of water and milk to reduce any unpleasant tang. Rinse and pat dry before cooking. Roasting the bird with a potato, or onion and garlic, inside can also improve the flavour.
- A spicy fruit chutney is a good accompaniment to roasted duck.

QUARTERING A DUCK

1 With the duck's tail farthest from you, run the knife alongside and through the breastbone from tail to neck. Fan the body open, skin side down.

2 Cut alongside and through the length of the spine. Use the weight in the heel of your hand on any particularly tough areas, such as the wishbone.

3 Lay one half of the duck skin side up and, holding the leg portion in your other hand, cut in two on a slight diagonal. Repeat with the other half.

Preparing and Jointing Pheasant

The pheasant is the most popular, accessible and versatile of all the game birds brought to the table. The large breasts can easily act as a substitute for chicken when used in most quick and easy recipes – perfect for when a midweek supper has to be on the table in around half an hour.

To ensure the maximum possible succulence, cook pheasant breasts with the moisture-trapping skin on, and keep them on the bone too. The breastbone acts as a superb heat conductor, helping the meat to cook evenly.

If you are cooking a whole pheasant, regular basting with butter is probably more important than a few pieces of bacon wrapped around a bird of this size. Resting time is also vitally important, as with any roast.

The pheasant's flavour will hold its own in traditional, slow-cooked recipes that ordinarily call for tough old chickens. For these you can joint the bird, as shown here. Another way to cook pheasant is to bone the legs for stuffing and rolling. Before you draw and joint the bird you will need to remove the feet as shown for duck on the previous pages.

▶ *Pheasant is particularly good when cooked with cream and mushrooms.*

1 Hold the bird breast-down and cut from the centre of the neck and away from you. Hold the neck skin and the crop in the left hand, pull the stump away from the crop and skin.

2 Cut through the neck stump, twist and remove it. Separate the windpipe from the skin of the neck and cut through it as close to the body as you can.

3 Push a finger through into the cavity where the neck was. Rotate the finger round to free the connective tissue holding the organs within the bird.

4 With the bird on its back, pinch the skin above the vent, and cut halfway through. Cut around the vent area, leaving this part perfectly intact.

5 Push two or three fingers into the bird and remove the contents in one motion. The kidneys will be retained inside. If cooking whole, your bird is now ready.

6 To remove the legs, cut down through the skin between the thigh and the breast section and pull the leg away from the body.

7 Flatten the thigh to allow the ball at the top of the femur to pop into view, sufficiently to dislocate the hip joint.

8 With your knife cut along the top of the thigh close to the body. Cut between the socket and the ball at the top of the femur.

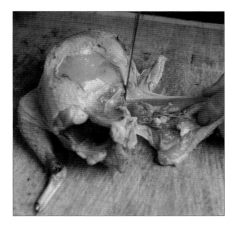

9 Continue on the same line, cutting as close to the body as possible to free the leg. Now repeat the process with the other leg.

10 To bone a leg for stuffing, cut through the tissue at the 'knee' joint. Gently cut the flesh on either side of the bone, then on the underside until the bone is free and can be pulled away.

Tips for Cooking Pheasant
- When selecting birds for the pot, avoid any with legs that have been badly damaged by shot, as these birds are likely to have punctured guts too, which will spoil them rapidly.
- When buying pheasant, look for a young cock, this will have small, blunt, rounded spurs on its legs. A cock bird in its second and third year will have longer, sharper spurs.
- When slow-cooking pheasant, always ensure that you remove the thigh tendons. Long cooking turns these into horrible little spikes with a texture similar to plastic.
- Generally, although smaller, younger hens are the best for roasting, younger cock birds will roast nicely enough if treated well, whereas older cock birds need slow-cooking methods, jointed as shown here, or are better suited mixed with other game for use in terrines, pâtés and salmis.
- Pheasant breasts poached in a little stock to retain their succulence are great to eat cold, sliced into finger-thin strips and coated with a good, fresh mayonnaise with a little chopped tarragon. Serve with baby spinach and some herby leaves.

Drawing and Filleting Goose

Whether your preference is for Canada, greylag or pinkfoot, the principles remain the same. Geese are hard work, but a young bird can be absolutely fantastic eating, not dissimilar to mallard. Duck and goose recipes are interchangeable, but one problem is finding casserole dishes and pans big enough to take a goose. Another point to consider is that wild geese offer very little meat for their total weight. A 3kg/7lb bird will probably just about feed four people.

Identifying the age of wild geese is notoriously difficult; size and weight is probably a good indicator if you have others to gauge it against. The old method of looking for a springy breastbone and youthful, unworn feet to identify a young bird is never more important than with a wild goose.

If you're not planning to roast your goose whole, you can fillet out the very generous breast steaks and either dice or slice them horizontally and flash-fry them. Asian flavours work very well with goose, as well as the earthy spices associated with cooked milk puddings, such as nutmeg, allspice and cinnamon.

▶ *Wild geese are not often available from game merchants, so the only way to obtain them is by shooting them.*

1 Holding the plucked bird breast down, run the knife up the back of the neck and away from you.

2 Use a cleaver or a heavy knife to remove the head and discard it.

3 Hold the neck skin and crop in one hand, pulling the neck stump away. Stretch the windpipe and gullet, and sever this close to the bird's body.

4 Instead of putting your fingers into the cavity, as with smaller birds, here you will need to run a knife around the cavity area to release the tissues connecting the organs to the body.

5 Turn the bird on to its back, pinch the skin at the tip of the breastbone, just above the vent, and cut down halfway, but not all the way through, to expose the bird's entrails.

6 Cut around the vent, leaving this section intact. Plugging the vent with some kitchen paper can help prevent the meat becoming tainted with guano.

7 Using the blade of a new garden trowel rather than your fingers, chisel through the fat deposits binding the contents to the inside of the bird.

8 Pull out the innards in one swift motion. Wipe the bird's cavity thoroughly with some kitchen paper or rinse through with water and dry.

9 Remove the feet with a blow from a cleaver or a heavy knife on each leg. If the bird is to be roasted whole, truss the legs with butcher's string.

FILLETING A GOOSE

1 Beginning at the bird's tail end and using the tip of the knife, slice down against the breastbone.

2 At the base of the wishbone, cut through the connective tendon and ease the breast away in one piece.

◀ **4** On the textured side of the main fillet, you'll notice a slightly glossy silver patch towards the rounder end of the triangular shape as you look down at it. Carefully cut this patch out, working from the outer edge inwards. As you do so, you'll find the shiny patch leads to a sheet of very tough tendon.

5 Gently scrape the meat away from the tendon, draw it out and discard it. The removal of this tough 'flight' tendon will ensure that the fillet stays flat when it's cooked. No matter what you do to a fillet that retains this tendon, it cannot be made tender, so it must be removed. Repeat the process with the remaining breast fillet.

3 With the fillet skin side down, remove the mini fillet by scraping out the tendon connecting it to the fillet. Then remove the other tendon running the length of the mini fillet, by anchoring the tendon and pushing the flesh away from you.

> **Tips for Cooking Wild Goose**
> • Pineapple juice helps to tenderize goose meat without imparting too much fruity flavour.
> • The breast fillets are very tasty if sliced horizontally, dipped in beaten egg and breadcrumbs and pan-fried like veal escalopes. Serve with lemon wedges.
> • Serve cold roast goose in thin slices accompanied by pickled pears and a soft blue cheese such as Roquefort, Picos or Gorgonzola.

Drawing and Trussing Turkey

The turkey is hunted for sport and for the table. Its foraging nature gives a wealth of texture to the flavours this meat can offer, but it also keeps the bird fit and lean and free of fat. Luckily, most recipes for farmed birds still cling to the idea that all turkeys are dry in texture, which can only assist the wild turkey hunter and cook.

If you decide to roast the whole bird, a good fatty pork-based stuffing will definitely help to lend it some moisture, as will regular basting during cooking. Roasting the bird supported upside down will also allow the fat from the stuffing to run into, and moisten, the breast area. Roughly speaking, a 4.5kg/10lb turkey will need around 1kg/2¼lb prepared stuffing.

▲ *Like most quarry species, wild turkey has much less fat than farmed birds.*

Tips for Cooking Wild Turkey

• To keep the breast as moist as possible, you can try working 200–250g/7–9oz cream cheese between the breast and the skin of the bird, working from the neck down. Herby cheeses work well – you could always add your own chopped herbs to a plain cheese. If the cheese is a little thick and unmanageable, loosen it with a splash of olive oil.

• The absence of fat in wild turkey can be overcome by twinning the meat with something fatty and tasty like pig's trotters (feet). They marry well together in casseroles.

1 Begin with the feet. Cut or score the skin between the foot and the knuckle joint with a cleaver or heavy knife.

2 Break the 'shin' bone in two. Cutting the leg here minimizes shrinkage and drying out during cooking.

3 Grip the foot in your hand, or in a wall-mounted v-brace, and pull to slowly draw out the tendons from the leg.

4 With the bird breast down, run the tip of the knife up the centre of the neck. Cut through to remove the head.

5 Holding the neck skin and crop in one hand, pull the neck stump away from it. A clean, damp towel can help your grip.

6 Cut through the neck stump, twist and remove it. The neck can be retained for making stock or gravy.

7 Carefully separate the windpipe from the skin of the neck. Stretching the windpipe and gullet, which is attached to the crop, cut through this as close to the bird's body as you can.

8 Push your fingers into the cavity where the neck has been removed. Rotating a knife instead of your fingers can help free any difficult connective tissue holding the organs within the bird.

9 With the bird on its back, pinch the skin close to the point of the breastbone, above the vent, and carefully cut down halfway – not all the way through – exposing the innards.

12 Wipe the cavity thoroughly with kitchen paper. If the drawing has been done correctly there should be no real need to rinse the bird's cavity, but if you suspect that the gut may have been torn or punctured by shot, it may be prudent to wash the cavity thoroughly with cold running water.

13 Pat the bird dry, inside and out. The kidneys will be retained inside the bird, either side of the backbone.

10 Carefully cut around the vent area, leaving this part perfectly intact. Plugging the vent with kitchen paper will help prevent any seepage and tainting.

11 Following the arc of the cavity along the inside of the breastbone, push one hand into the bird and remove all the contents in one smooth motion.

TRUSSING A TURKEY

1 Trussing the bird gives it a neat shape for roasting. Cut a length of butcher's string about 75cm/30in long and pass this under the legs.

2 Knot the string in the middle, on top of the legs. Pull the two ends tight and then pass them between the legs and the tail, or parson's nose.

3 Turn the bird over on to its breast. Pass each end of the string under and past each leg, finishing under each wing. Pull tight, knot and trim the ends.

Fire-baked Partridge in a Crust

This recipe, ideal for the open air, has its roots in an ancient technique used by Romany gypsies for cooking hedgehogs, as it assisted in stripping off the spines. Here the hedgehog is replaced with a partridge, cooked in an edible flour and water paste. You will need a good fire to create lots of embers.

Serves 1

1 partridge, plucked, drawn and gutted
¼ lemon
1 garlic clove
1 rosemary sprig
500g/1¼lb/5 cups plain
    (all-purpose) flour
sea salt and ground black pepper

For the ratatouille

1 courgette (zucchini), sliced
1 red (bell) pepper, sliced
1 onion, chopped
a few basil leaves
3 fresh or canned tomatoes, chopped
sea salt and ground black pepper

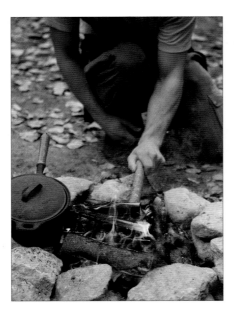

1 First build up the fire so that you will have a good pile of hot embers.

2 Season the cavity of the partridge with salt and pepper and stuff with the lemon, garlic and rosemary. Push the legs down beside the body. Season the skin of the bird with salt and pepper.

3 To make the dough, place the flour and 5ml/1 tsp salt in a plastic bag and add 300ml/1½ pint/1¼ cups water.

4 Knead the flour and water together through the bag; add a further 300ml/½ pint/1¼ cups water and repeat to make a pliable dough. Add more water if necessary, but don't make it too wet.

5 Spread out a double thickness of foil approximately 45cm/18in square and place the dough in the centre. Using your hands, spread the dough into a circle 2.5cm/1in thick.

6 Place the bird in the centre of the dough and encase it completely by pulling up each side of the dough and pressing the edges together to seal.

7 Pull up the foil on both sides, roll them together down towards the bird, then draw up the ends and scrunch together. Wrap the bird in a second piece of foil.

8 Place the package in the embers of the fire for 5 minutes, turn it through 180 degrees for 10 minutes then move it back to its original position. Surround the bird with embers and leave for 30 minutes. Remove from the fire and allow to cool for at least 15 minutes.

9 Meanwhile, place the ratatouille ingredients on a double layer of foil, season with salt and pepper, then drizzle with plenty of olive oil. Fold the foil to create a second parcel. Place in the fire with the partridge and cook for 30 minutes.

10 To serve the partridge, fold back the foil and cut into the crust with a sharp knife, cutting outwards away from the meat. If you wish you can scoop out the interior of the dough to eat with it. Serve with the ratatouille.

Energy 969kcal/4055kJ; Protein 129.2g; Carbohydrate 31.3g, of which sugars 27.1g; Fat 36.9g, of which saturates 8.1g; Cholesterol 0mg; Calcium 266mg; Fibre 8.2g; Sodium 357mg

Poached Partridge

This simple dish has its origins in the Austro-Hungarian region and can easily be prepared and cooked in the field, as it needs only one pot and an open fire with a trivet. The partridges are gently poached in beer with vegetables and dried sour cherries, which give the gravy a distinctive flavour.

Serves 4

75g/3oz/6 tbsp duck fat or lard
4 partridges, plucked, drawn
   and cleaned
1 medium onion, chopped
2 medium carrots, diced
1 celery stick, chopped
2 medium leeks, sliced
6 garlic cloves, sliced
1 litre/1¾ pints/4 cups hoppy beer
1 bay leaf
50g/2oz dried sour cherries
675g/1½lb waxy potatoes, cut into
   1cm/½in dice
sea salt and ground black pepper
rye bread, to serve

1 Heat a pan just big enough to hold the birds side by side without squashing them. Add the fat and melt, then brown the birds on all sides.

2 Add the onion, carrots, celery and leeks to the pan and cook, stirring, until softened.

3 Add the sliced garlic to the pan, then pour in the beer.

4 Add the bay leaf and cherries, season with salt and pepper and bring to a simmer, but heat gently, otherwise the birds might toughen.

5 Once the liquid is simmering, cover and cook gently for 15 minutes.

6 When they are cooked, remove the partridges from the pan and keep warm.

7 Add the potatoes to the pan, and boil until tender. Return the partridges to the pot to warm. Serve with rye bread.

Energy 866kcal/3642kJ; Protein 124.5g; Carbohydrate 39.1g, of which sugars 13.6g; Fat 24.3g, of which saturates 6.3g; Cholesterol 0mg; Calcium 184mg; Fibre 2.9g; Sodium 369mg

Duck Liver Salad

It is preferable to gut your kill as soon as possible, and it therefore makes sense to make the offal your first meal. The liver of game birds cooks quickly and has a great, rich taste, so this is an ideal dish for cooking outside for a hunter's lunch.

Serves 4

25g/1oz/2 tbsp lard or olive oil
225g/8oz smoked streaky (fatty) bacon
    or pancetta, diced
2 garlic cloves, cut in half lengthways
2 good handfuls mixed salad leaves
2 thick slices of bread cut into
    1cm/½in cubes
12 duck livers
30ml/2 tbsp balsamic vinegar
sea salt and ground black pepper

1 Heat a large frying pan over medium heat and add the fat and bacon. Cook gently until the bacon is browned on all sides and the fat has run from it.

2 Remove the bacon from the pan, leaving the rendered fat behind. Set the bacon aside.

3 Add the garlic to the pan and cook until golden; remove from the pan and reserve this also.

4 Place a handful of salad leaves on each of four serving plates and season with salt and pepper.

Variations Try this recipe with venison or wild boar liver – simply slice the liver into 1cm/½in pieces. Alternatively, use a mix of different bird or rabbit livers. You can also try replacing the bacon with chorizo and using pre-cooked diced potatoes instead of the bread.

5 Add the bread cubes to the pan, season with a little salt and pepper and fry gently until golden and crisp before dividing between the serving plates.

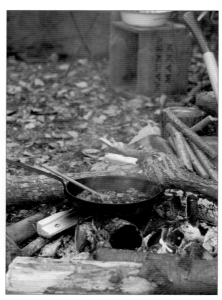

6 Move the pan to the hottest part of the fire, season the livers and put them into the hot pan. Use tongs if you have them, as the liver may spit explosively when it hits the hot fat.

7 Cook quickly for 1 minute, then turn the livers and cook for 1 minute more. Return the bacon and garlic to the pan. Pour in the vinegar and allow to sizzle then turn the livers in the juices before distributing the contents equally among the waiting salads.

Energy 344kcal/1435kJ; Protein 21g; Carbohydrate 13.5g, of which sugars 1.5g; Fat 21.3g, of which saturates 8.3g; Cholesterol 232mg; Calcium 49mg; Fibre 0.8g; Sodium 883mg

Outdoor Duck and Bean Casserole

The sight of a bubbling pot of beans will warm the soul of the coldest of hunters. This dish gains an extra dimension from the addition of a hoppy pilsner beer from the Czech Republic such as Pilsner Urquell, Budvar or Gambrinus. Using whole ducks requires you to cut the breasts off the bone and the legs from the carcasses, which can be added to the stew for extra flavour. You will need a casserole or stew pan that can be used directly on an open fire or suspended over one by its handle.

Serves 3–4

2 ducks, plucked and cleaned
50g/2oz/4 tbsp lard or beef dripping
225g/8oz smoked streaky (fatty)
   bacon, diced
2 medium onions, diced
6 garlic cloves, cut in half lengthways
2 bay leaves
2 rosemary or thyme sprigs
400g/14oz carton passata (bottled,
   strained tomatoes) or can tomatoes
2 x 330ml bottles Pilsner beer
2 x 400g/14oz cans white
   beans, drained
sea salt and ground black pepper
3 gherkins, sliced, and crusty bread
   to serve

1 To prepare the duck, first remove the legs by cutting between the thigh and carcass through the hip joint (if you first bend the leg back to dislocate the joint the job will be easier).

2 To remove the breasts, cut down either side of the breastbone to the ribcage, re-angle the knife and cut over the ribcage. Season all the pieces with salt and pepper.

Variations All game birds will work in this recipe but the cooking time required for the leg meat will vary. Diced boar or venison shoulder can also be used instead of duck.

3 Warm the pan and add the fat. When it has melted add the duck and fry over medium heat for 3 minutes each side. Remove the breasts and reserve.

4 Add the bacon to the pan and cook, stirring, for 3–5 minutes to release the fat before adding the onions and garlic. Fry, stirring, until the onions have softened, then add the pieces of fried duck.

5 Add the tomatoes, the herbs and the beer, and bring to the boil.

6 Move the pan to a less intense part of the fire and simmer gently, stirring occasionally, for 45–60 minutes, or until the leg meat is tender.

7 Add the beans to the pan, season with salt and pepper and bring back to a simmer.

8 Slice the reserved duck breasts and return to the pan to heat through. Serve the duck and beans immediately in big bowls, topped with some sliced gherkins and accompanied by chunks of crusty bread.

Energy 1023kcal/4270kJ; Protein 73g; Carbohydrate 31.8g, of which sugars 9.2g; Fat 63.5g, of which saturates 22.1g; Cholesterol 374mg; Calcium 94mg; Fibre 10.1g; Sodium 1749mg

Flame-cooked Pheasant on a Stick

Kebabs are a fabulously quick and easy way to cook meat outdoors. You will need two sticks about 30cm/12in long, preferably cut from a fruit tree such as cherry, apple or peach. Avoid pine, as the sap can have an overpowering flavour. Cook the kebabs over a barbecue or a small fire with a trivet.

Serves 2

4 pheasant breasts cut crossways into
    strips 1cm/½in wide
8 rashers (strips) of rindless streaky
    (fatty) bacon
100g/3¾oz couscous
15ml/1 tbsp olive oil
sea salt and ground black pepper
apple chutney, to serve

1 Find two suitable sticks to make the skewers. Cut off the leaves and sideshoots and strip away the bark. Sharpen one end of each to a point.

2 With a pushing and turning action, feed the end of a rasher of bacon on to it, starting about 2cm/¾in from the end. Spear a piece of pheasant on to the stick and lap the bacon round it.

Cook's tip Green wood is better than seasoned wood for the skewers, as it won't char so easily. If the sticks are dry, soak them for a few minutes after you have peeled off the bark.

3 Push down and repeat with more pieces of pheasant until half of the meat is on the skewer, with the bacon weaving in between.

4 Repeat the process with the other stick and the remaining pieces of bacon and pheasant.

5 Meanwhile, put the couscous in a bowl with 5ml/1 tsp of the olive oil and just cover with boiling water. Cover and leave for 5 minutes for the grains to swell, then fluff with a fork and season with salt and pepper.

6 Lightly coat the kebabs in the remaining olive oil and season with salt and pepper. Place on the grill rack, cook for 3–5 minutes, turn over and cook for a further 3–5 minutes.

7 Turn the kebabs again and cook for a further 2 minutes on each side. The meat should be cooked thoroughly and the bacon fat sizzling, but check by cutting into a piece of pheasant before eating. Serve with the couscous and some apple chutney on the side.

Variation Any of the small game birds, as well as rabbit and squirrel loins, can replace the pheasant.

Pheasant Cooked on a Cider Can

One of the best ways to cook a bird in the field is on top of a can of cider or beer. This may sound bizarre but placing the pheasant – or any bird – on top of a half-full can of beer or cider, then sealing the pot, creates a high-pressure steamer that keeps the pheasant incredibly moist. It is also an ideal cooking method for an overnight hunting trip when you want to take a minimal amount of equipment.

Serves 2

1 cock pheasant, drawn and cleaned
2 x 500ml/17fl oz cans (hard) cider
1 rosemary sprig
1 bay leaf
sea salt and ground black pepper
fresh thyme sprigs, to garnish
   (optional)
crusty bread, to serve

1 Truss the bird through the crown and drumsticks to prevent the legs dropping and touching the bottom of the pan.

2 Season the pheasant inside and out. Open one can of cider and pour half into the pan. Add another 275ml/9fl oz/ 1 cup from the other can to the pan.

Cook's tip You could seal the pan with a flour and water crust instead of foil. Mix flour and water in a bag to a soft dough, place around the rim of the pan then press the lid down firmly.

3 Place the rosemary and bay leaf (or any herbs that are to hand) in the half-full can of cider.

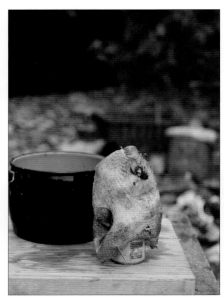

4 Sit the pheasant firmly on the can, making sure it is pushed down far enough to stay upright, then carefully place the assembly in the centre of the pan.

5 Cover the pan with a triple layer of foil. Don't pull the foil tight but mound it over the top so that it traps air inside and doesn't touch the bird.

6 Place the pan over the hottest part of the fire and cook for 4–6 minutes, then draw it back so it is half in the flames and cook for 1 hour, turning regularly.

7 Remove the pan from the heat and leave for 15–30 minutes so that the pressure drops and the meat rests.

8 Lift off the bird and discard the can. Strip the meat from the bones and add it to the juices in the pan. Sprinkle with thyme, and serve with crusty bread.

Energy 547kcal/2287kJ; Protein 58g; Carbohydrate 6.6g, of which sugars 6.6g; Fat 24.8g, of which saturates 8.4g; Cholesterol 460mg; Calcium 80mg; Fibre 0g; Sodium 154mg

Field Casserole of Pheasant, Prunes and Rioja

The flavour of the cock pheasant is already strong so there is no real need to hang it, making this recipe perfect for cooking in the field. An older pheasant requires a slower cooking method and can take some strong flavours. The use of Spain's most famous red wine, Rioja, gives this casserole a rich flavour and is a great foil for the deep, rounded sweetness of the prunes. You will need a heavy pan with a lid, and you can cook the casserole on either an open fire or a portable stove.

Serves 2

50g/2oz/4 tbsp lard or duck fat
1 pheasant, drawn, cleaned
  and jointed
1 medium onion, chopped
1 large carrot, diced
1 celery stick, sliced
4 garlic cloves, sliced
1 leek, cleaned and shredded
1 bay leaf
2.5ml/½ tsp dried oregano or thyme
½ bottle Rioja
1 chicken stock (bouillon) cube
12 pitted prunes
sea salt and ground black pepper
boiled rice or crusty bread, to serve

1 Warm the pan on the fire and add the fat. Season the pheasant pieces and add to the pan, allowing them to sizzle in the fat for 2 minutes.

2 Add the chopped onion and diced carrot to the pheasant.

3 Continue to cook, stirring, for 6–8 minutes, until the meat and vegetables have all begun to brown.

4 Add the celery, sliced garlic and shredded leek to the pan and continue to cook for a further 5–6 minutes, stirring occasionally.

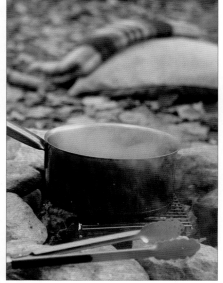

5 When all the vegetables have softened and cooked down, add the herbs to the pan, together with the wine, the stock cube and a little more seasoning. Bring to the boil then draw the pan to the edge of the fire, where the heat is less intense, and leave to simmer gently for 20 minutes.

6 Add a little more liquid if necessary during cooking, or cover the pan if the casserole is bubbling too fiercely.

7 Add the prunes and continue to cook gently for 30 minutes. By this time the meat should be very tender and falling off the bones.

8 Serve the casserole in bowls, piping hot, with some rice or some good, crusty bread to help absorb the juices.

Energy 959kcal/3997kJ; Protein 63g; Carbohydrate 35.8g, of which sugars 32.6g; Fat 50.7g, of which saturates 18.8g; Cholesterol 483mg; Calcium 161mg; Fibre 8.4g; Sodium 187mg

Turkey Saltimbocca

Saltimbocca translates as 'jump in the mouth' and refers to the burst of flavours delivered when you eat this. A truly Italian dish originally made with veal, cured ham and sage with a zingy lemon finish, this recipe can be utilized to suit most white poultry and meat as well as fish. It is simple and quick to cook, making it ideal for serving in the field. The salad can be prepared in advance at home.

Serves 4

15ml/1 tbsp olive oil
8 x 75g/3oz turkey escalopes, cut through their length and lightly batted with the heel of the hand until 6mm/⅓in thick
8 basil leaves
175g/6oz/¾ cup butter
8 slices prosciutto
1 lemon, halved
sea salt and ground black pepper

For the salad

4 baby potatoes, boiled, cooled and halved
225g/8oz jar roasted red (bell) peppers
225g/8oz fine green beans, blanched and cooled
20 pitted black olives
20 basil leaves, torn
60ml/4 tbsp extra virgin olive oil
15ml/1 tbsp balsamic vinegar
sea salt and ground black pepper

1 To make the salad, mix all the ingredients except the balsamic vinegar in a bowl, season, mix well, cover and set aside. If you make the salad at home, mix it in a large plastic container so it is easy to carry.

Variation Wild boar loin or pheasant breast will work very well in this recipe in place of the turkey.

2 Top each escalope with a basil leaf. Place a 15g/½oz pat of butter over the leaf and lay a slice of prosciutto across the centre of the turkey, over the butter.

3 Fold the two ends of the proscuitto tightly under the escalope. Season with plenty of pepper and a little salt. Repeat with the remaining turkey escalopes.

4 Heat a large frying pan over a hot fire, add the oil and heat until it begins to smoke. Quickly add the turkey parcels, basil and butter side down.

5 Cook the escalopes hard and fast to crisp the proscuitto. When nicely coloured (approximately 2 minutes) turn the escalopes to cook the other side.

6 As they sizzle, add the remaining butter and allow it to melt and foam before squeezing all the juice from the lemon into the pan. Give the pan a good shake to combine the meat juices, melted butter and lemon juice. Remove from the heat and allow to rest.

7 Dress the salad with the balsamic vinegar, toss well to combine, then serve with the escalopes, with the pan juices drizzled over the top.

Energy 616kcal/2550kJ; Protein 22.5g; Carbohydrate 13.6g, of which sugars 5.5g; Fat 52.8g, of which saturates 26.3g; Cholesterol 145mg; Calcium 47mg; Fibre 3g; Sodium 800mg

VENISON

The various deer species offer the cook a wonderfully low-fat meat with hardly any wastage at all. There is a cut for every need: minced or ground meat from the shin and shoulder for the healthiest of burgers and cottage pies, large joints such as the shoulder or haunch for family gatherings, and the melt-in-the-mouth fillet and strip loin for that special dinner.

Offal, such as the heart and liver, still suffers a little from a lingering culinary stigma; you either love it or hate it, but we hope you'll be brave enough to try our suggestions and recipes. The butchery of such a large animal can appear daunting, but you may find satisfaction in the process once you begin, and with this step-by-step guide, in time – with practice – you'll undoubtedly become quicker and more proficient.

◄ *If you are planning a weekend of hunting and cooking, don't feel you need to take more than a few well chosen ingredients and utensils for creating the most delicious dishes.*

Preparing Small Deer

Treat venison as well as you can and you will be repaid ten times over by this wonderfully delicious, versatile and incredibly healthy red meat.

Most people who have been put off 'overhung' venison have probably tasted meat spoilt by too high a hanging temperature and lingering blood contamination. The optimum temperature for the hanging of deer is just a little above freezing at 2°C/35°F. This applies whether you have a purpose-built deer larder or have simply customized an old refrigerator. For small deer such as roe, muntjac and the smaller varieties of whitetail, one to two weeks' hanging time is plenty.

Most cuts of smaller, younger deer roast beautifully, and the simplest hedgerow accompaniments are the best things to really show this meat off. Any fruit that makes a jam or chutney will almost certainly work served alongside venison or worked into the gravy. The old Italian trick of whisking a little bitter dark (bittersweet) chocolate into the gravy to finish it probably works better with venison than with anything else.

▶ *Venison offers the game cook a huge assortment of culinary possibilities.*

GUTTING A SMALL (ROE) DEER

1 To bleed a freshly shot deer, run the tip of your knife along the jawline to a depth of about 1cm/½in – enough to nick the carotid artery. Keep the body above the head. The slope of a hillside helps any blood to drain freely away.

2 Once the blood has drained off (how long this takes depends on its size), turn the roe on to its back so that the stomach is exposed and the legs splay outwards. Make a cut in front of the penis sheath or female genitals.

3 Using small nicking cuts, work each side of the sheath, pulling it back towards the pelvis. This will eventually open up access to an inverted v-shape, which forms part of the pelvis.

4 Work the knife down the insides of the v-shape, making sure you do not cut into any of the softer tissues below the skin line, until the rectum and anal canal can be seen. Work a finger underneath to loosen any connecting tissues.

5 Proceed in this way until your blade can easily follow this path. Then cut down on to the tail bone, severing any final connecting fibres. The anus and lower intestinal canal can now be freed in one, completely intact.

6 Take care when making the initial incision; the flesh is very thin and you must avoid cutting into the stomach and risking contamination. Cover the point of your knife with your finger to prevent it cutting deeper than you intend.

7 With your knife point covered with your pointing finger, run the blade up to the sternum. End the cut at the natural apex of the ribcage.

8 Once you've reached the breastbone, you will no longer be able to keep your finger in place. Carry on with the blade, working up to just under the chin.

9 You will now have exposed the white ribbed windpipe and the thinner, darker upper digestive tract, which need to be separated. Avoid puncturing the latter.

10 Using a fine-toothed saw for the breastbone, saw through it to meet the windpipe. Once the ribcage is open, use your knife to clear away any connecting membranes in this area.

11 Returning to the tail end of the deer, gather the stomach and entire contents up towards the neck end to give your hand enough room as you return to work around the pelvis.

12 The entire section encompassing the rectum, penis and testes can now be pushed through the v-shaped cavity to join the stomach and the rest of the body contents.

13 The extra space you've created will make it easier to retrieve the deer's kidneys, located against the back of the cavity wall. Check the removed kidneys for any spots, cysts or blisters and any pale scarring.

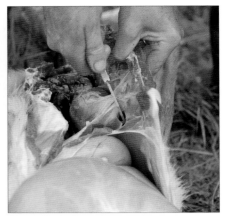

14 Now the diaphragm can be freed from both sides of the ribcage. Trim this membrane away from the ribs and down each side to the spine. The diaphragm will come away when the heart, lungs and liver are removed.

15 Having 'rolled' the cavity contents up towards the head, use short nicking strokes and a firm, even pull to sever any connective tissue along the spine. Once all tissues connecting the body contents are severed, roll them up.

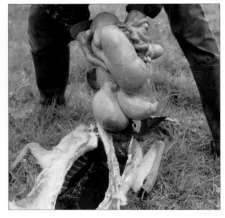

16 The entire body contents are now free except for the connection at the windpipe and upper digestive tract. They can be pulled free of the body to come to rest alongside the deer.

Checking Internal Organs

Once the internal organs have been removed, you must inspect them carefully for any signs of abnormality, as detailed below. If anything gives you cause for concern, the internal organs and the stomach should be bagged and labelled. Do not eat any of the deer until you have spoken to someone in authority at your local government agricultural health department. The carcass may have to be taken away and analysed if there is any sign of infection. If you feel the deer is generally in a poor state of health, it is best discarded as unfit for human consumption. You never really know what you may encounter until the animal is felled. Whenever handling the meat and internal organs of wild deer, wear long protective gloves if you are inexperienced.
• Check the lungs for grey patches, cysts or scar tissue.
• Lymph glands should be small and pale. Look out for discharges or if they are dark and enlarged.
• The liver should be a smooth gelatinous mass, without any hard areas, discoloration or lumps.
• The heart and kidneys should be free of scarring, cysts or blisters.
• It is prudent to check with your own local deerstalking bodies and agricultural bodies for general advice and best practice approach to the treatment of lymph glands and offal.

◄**17** Sever these last tubes as close to the base of the tongue as possible. This will reduce the risk of contamination from food matter. Any obvious food in the throat can be 'milked' or squeezed down towards the gut before severing the tube. Now cut away the liver, kidneys and heart.

18 ►Turn the carcass over to help any remaining blood drain away.

SKINNING SMALL DEER

1 Make a small slit between the foot and the hock joint, in the gap between the bone and the ligament, on both hind legs. Insert a gambrel and suspend.

2 Run the knife up from the middle of the deer's thigh to the hock joint. Cut around the joint, working the skin away. Avoid cutting the tendon at all costs.

3 Repeat this process with the second leg, then work the skin away from around the tail; cut through the tail, leaving it attached to the skin.

4 With both hands, or one hand and gentle nicking cuts with your knife, work the skin gently away from the body down towards the neck.

5 Once you have skinned the flanks you'll have to use only your knife to carefully cut around the shoulders. If the deer is female, remove the udder.

6 To skin the forelegs, run your knife tip from the joint closest to the foot up to the skinned shoulder area, then free any remaining skin from around the neck.

7 Remove the head by locating the notch at the base of the skull and cutting through this.

8 To remove the feet, find the notch on the joint, work your knife into the gap, and cut through the connective tissue.

▲ *From nose to tail, deer offer a wealth of opportunities for the cook, and there is rarely much wastage.*

SMALL DEER BUTCHERY

1 To separate the fore-end from the rib section: with the deer on its side, neck on the left, locate the tip of the shoulder blade with the tip of your knife.

2 Cut down through the fore-end to the spine. With your saw, cut through the backbone. Complete the cut with a knife to sever the fore-end.

3 You can now cut the thin shanks or forelegs from both front legs. These can be reserved for stock.

4 Remove the breast sections by cutting from the thin end of the flank where it joins the haunch until you meet the ribs.

5 You will be able to cut through only half of this section with your knife; use a saw to cut through the rib area.

6 Trim out the lymph glands on each side. Wipe the cavity free of any bone dust and blood.

7 Remove the saddle from the haunch: cut down from the tip of the hip, then directly across. Sever the spine with a saw then finish with the knife.

8 You may wish to cut off some of the rib length. Cut through the rib sections on either side with a cleaver or saw. Try to keep the blade parallel to the spine.

▲ *The finished saddle, ready for cooking.*

9 To retrieve the two fillets either side of the saddle, run the knife tip along the spine, following the bone edge to guide you and using short nicking strokes.

10 Once the fillets are free of the bone, trim away any silvery sheets of tendon covering the fillets and the long 'chain' of gristle running the length of each fillet.

11 Turning the saddle over, concentrate now on the fleshier end of the spine. Carefully cut out the tenderloins on either side. Trim out any sinew.

12 These tiny fillets can be cut in half horizontally, but not all the way through – about 90 per cent – then opened out and carefully beaten flat.

13 Now turn to the haunch. To separate the legs, cut down through the middle of the haunch with a knife until you reach the pelvis. Carry on through the bone with a saw, then cut through the remaining flesh with your knife. Trim and tidy away any silvery tendons, bone dust and fragments.

16 Once you've cut around the ball in the socket of the joint and the two are separate, continue with your knife, using short scraping strokes, following to the end of the bone.

17 Again, working on the flat side of the pelvic bone, but this time under the socket, continue the same line as before to free the bone.

14 For presentation purposes, you may wish to remove the shank or simply 'knuckle' it by partially cutting through the joint and bending it back on the leg.

15 Remove the halved section of pelvis, cutting along the flat side of the pelvis with the cut side away from you, edging your knife towards the ball of the femur.

18 Remove any obvious sinews or tendons and the lymph gland (indicated).

19 Remove the femur from the leg, by nicking away any connective tissues around the round head of the bone.

20 With long strokes, run the blade of a hambone gouge along the length of all faces of the femur, away from the head.

21 Repeat the process at the other end, by chipping around the end of the bone with the knife tip. Then push the femur through the tunnel you've made.

22 To finish boning the leg properly, remove the last piece of knee-cap remaining. This is easily identified as a small, white, dish-like cap of bone.

Tips for Cooking Small Deer

• The fresh liver of a young deer shot in the early hours is widely considered as the stalker's breakfast treat. Slice it thinly and fry gently in a little oil and butter with a scant sprinkling of finely chopped sage. Serve with grilled bacon and tomatoes, eggs, fried bread and a few wild mushrooms.

• The loin, cut into thick coins, offers a stunning dish if seared in a smoking hot pan for a minute or so each side. Serve with anything from green beans, fried potatoes and Béarnaise sauce to a salad with a sharp raspberry vinaigrette.

• The sheet of caul fat from the inside of the deer helps keep lean joints moist while cooking. Use it to wrap haunches, saddles or shoulder joints. Thinly sliced pancetta or good quality streaky (fatty) bacon works well too.

• The slightly bitter leaves of chicory (Belgian endive) make an unusual and quite superb addition to any roasted venison dish. Either braise the chicory leaves in a little game or chicken stock, or steam them for about 15 minutes. Drain them thoroughly, dredge them with sugar, salt and pepper and pan-fry them to colour and crisp them up.

▲ *A whole leg ready for cooking. The string helps keeps the meat tender.*

▲ *Venison benefits from being enclosed in a layer of pancetta or fatty bacon.*

▲ *A boned leg will need less cooking time than if the bone is left in place.*

Preparing Large Deer

Ideally, for optimum tenderness and flavour, the larger species of deer can hang in your cold store for a week or two. Three weeks is probably a little too long unless you enjoy gamey venison. The ideal temperature is just above freezing at 2°C/35°F.

Take a little time and care over the preparation of your kill and you'll be repaid with the most majestic of game meats. Wild venison is much healthier than most other red meats, rich in omega-3, low in cholesterol and free of any growth promoters. The warming heartiness of deer can be accentuated with beefy red wine sauces, but it also works well in delicately spiced dishes.

▶ *Venison has a huge amount of flavour, and is the king of game dishes.*

GUTTING LARGE DEER

1 All shot deer should be thoroughly bled. Place one foot on the neck and push the knife into the point just above the breastbone. Twist the knife through a quarter-turn and leave it in place.

2 Pushing down on the shoulder and ribs can help force the blood out. When the blood has drained off, make a small slit between the deer's foot and the hock joint on both hind legs.

3 The holes should be made in the gap between the bone and the Achilles tendon. Insert the gambrel and hang the deer at a comfortable height so you can work easily.

4 Remove the hind legs by finding the notch at the hock joint and working your knife into the gap, cutting through the connective tissue. Push the leg back to dislocate the joint and cut away. Repeat with the front legs, cutting through the notch between hoof and first joint.

5 If preparing a buck, hold the penis in one hand, cut around this and up to and around the scrotum. Remove the genitals, male or female, from their location and lay them, still attached, down near the tail.

6 Now, with your fingers hooking the flesh away from the stomach sac, cut down until you reach the breastbone. The curved or slightly hooked blade of a carpet-fitter's knife (or craft knife), rather than a butcher's knife, may assist you in not cutting too deeply.

7 Returning to the tail end, saw through the pelvis to allow the carcass to cool. Move behind the carcass. Continue the cut from the genitals around the anus.

8 Complete the cut under the tail. The genitals and various tubes should be in one hand as you cut with the other. Now return to the front of the deer.

9 The stomach sac will fall forward to give access to the lower intestines. Cut at the point indicated to allow the loose section to drop clear of the cavity.

◄ **10** Returning to the pelvis, cut the connecting tissues under the bladder, making sure you do not nick through the bladder or any of the tubing. Once released, push this through the gap you've created to join the other organs and the section of lower intestine. The whole collection of organs should come away in one section, perhaps with a little help from your knife near to the tail.

11 ► Turning your attention to the breastbone, run your saw down through the sternum. Pull out the caul fat.

12 You will now be able to remove the highest positioned kidney, located on the back wall of the cavity. The second kidney will be just slightly lower down. To free the lungs, heart and other organs in the chest area, carefully nick away the diaphragm from each side of the cavity walls.

13 Now cut down and beyond the voice box of the deer, then sever the windpipe and upper digestive tract as high into the throat as possible, close to the tongue. If any food matter is present inside the digestive tract, 'milk' it toward the body and away from the point of severance before making the cut.

14 Finally, remove the head by cutting through the notch between the spine and the base of the skull. Moving the head up and down will assist you in getting the blade into the correct place. Removing the head at this point will preserve as much of the precious neck meat as possible.

SKINNING LARGE DEER

1 Run the knife from the middle of the deer's thigh up to and just beyond the hock joint. Using short, nicking strokes, cut away the skin around the hock joint.

2 Repeat this process with the other leg, working the skin away from the back of the legs and the flanks with short sweeping strokes of the knife.

3 When you reach the tail area, cut through the base of the tail bone. The tail should come away with the skin in one large section.

4 With both hands, work the skin gently away from the body down toward the neck. The age of the deer, body fat content and temperature will all affect how easily the skin is removed. Use your knife to help if necessary.

5 Once you reach the shoulders and forelegs, you'll have to use your knife to carefully cut around this slightly more complicated area. Use cautious, small cuts, and remove as little flesh as possible throughout the process.

6 ◀ To skin the foreleg, run your knife tip from the first joint closest to the hoof up to meet the skinned shoulder area. Gently free any skin from around the neck. Repeat to skin the second foreleg.

▶ *A deer hung for two weeks at around 2°C/35°F will produce superbly flavoursome, tender venison.*

> **Checking Internal Organs**
> Inspect the organs for any signs of abnormality, as for small deer.

LARGE DEER BUTCHERY

Before you begin to butcher a large deer, remove the lower legs and feet if you did not do this in the field. This is an ideal time to pick over the carcass, trim away any remaining skin patches and look for any darkened patches of meat, where blood has pooled during hanging. Cut away and discard anything that looks unpalatable.

▶ *A fallow deer carcass; fresh from a cold store, ready for butchering.*

1 To prepare the neck chops, trim off the end of the neck and any dried blood patches that have accumulated while hanging. Make three even scores down to the neck bone with your knife.

2 Using the knife marks as your guide, follow these cuts with a saw. Once through the bone, continue the cut with the knife. These neck chops are ideal for stewing, casseroling or braising.

3 Now cut the breast sections from the thin end of the flank where it joins the haunch from the ribs. Run the knife from the inner part of the top of the thigh along the flank towards the loin area.

4 You will be able to cut through only half of this section with your knife. The remaining section will need to be sawn through, following the same straight line with the saw.

5 Turn over and repeat the process with the other flank. Trim out any dried blood, any very dark and dry flesh or anything that looks unpleasant inside the cavity, including the lymph glands on each side. Wipe the cavity clear of any bone dust from the saw.

6 Now separate the shoulder section/ fore-end from the rib section. As you look down at the deer on its side, with the neck to your left, run your knife down to the spine between the sixth and seventh rib.

7 Mirror this cut between ribs six and seven on the opposite side of the ribcage. Saw through the backbone, then finish the sawn cut with your knife.

8 Be sure to remove the blade bones from the cut side of the rib section on both sides.

9 Trim out and dispose of any lymph glands and dark patches from the underside of the rib section.

10 To remove the saddle from the haunch, locate the gap near the end of the pelvic bone. Score from this point to the front of the body.

11 Cut the scored line until you hit the spine. Ignoring the spine for now, keep cutting through the line opposite. Then sever the spine with the saw.

12 Saw through the rib sections on either side, keeping the blade parallel to the spine, about 5cm/2in from it. The removed ribs can be used for stock.

▲ *A pristine saddle from a fallow deer, with a generous covering of protective fat. This prime cut will roast beautifully as a single joint.*

13 To make chops from the loin or saddle, split the spine down the middle vertically, beginning at the opposite end to the ribs. Use your saw for this part.

14 If you prefer, you can finish splitting the spine in half with a cleaver. Next, using the ribs to guide you, cut down through the flesh to the bone.

15 Finish the knife cuts you've made to cut through the spine with the cleaver. You should get more than 20 chops from the whole saddle.

16 Separate the legs with your knife and saw by completing the cut through the pelvis you made in the field. Trim and tidy away any tendons and bone dust.

17 For presentation purposes, you may wish to remove the shank, or simply 'knuckle' it by partially cutting through the joint and bending it back on the leg.

18 Trim and tidy away any very dark patches of flesh and fat, including the pronounced corner piece which harbours yet more lymph glands.

▲ *The haunch of venison can be simply roasted on the bone, but boned and stuffed it can't fail to impress.*

19 Remove the aitch bone by cutting along the flat side of the pelvis. Keeping the cut side of the bone nearest you, edge the knife along to expose the ball.

20 Once you've cut around the ball in the socket, it is separate from the joint. Continue to cut, with short scraping strokes, to the end of the bone.

21 Working on the flat side of the pelvic bone, but under the socket, continue the same line as before to free the bone. Remove tendons and the lymph gland.

22 With the femur head uppermost on your left as you look down, cut through the joint evenly at 2–3cm/¾–1¼in intervals to make four steaks.

23 To remove the femur from the leg, first ensure that the shank is removed by finding the notch with your knife. Cut the shank away through this point.

24 Nick away any connective tissues around the head of the femur. Run a hambone gouge down all 'faces' of the femur, away from the head.

25 At the other end of the bone, repeat the process by cutting around the end of the bone. The femur can now be pushed through the tunnel you've made.

26 To finish boning the leg properly, remove the last piece of knee-cap remaining. Trim away any very dark and dry patches on the leg.

▲ *It is well worth the effort of learning to string a joint of venison properly.*

27 To obtain three joints from the other leg, remove the shank, aitch bone and rump steaks as before. Place the leg with the tip of the femur away from you.

28 Run the knife tip along the thin seam of fat to part the muscle. Continue cutting, in long sweeping strokes, down towards the femur.

29 As you cut around the femur, you'll reveal another seam of muscle edged in a silvery membrane. Remove this muscle at this point.

30 Returning to the section with the bone still in place, gently cut away the flesh surrounding the femur.

31 Once all the flesh has been cut away you can ease the bone from the joint.

32 Now divide the boned joint into two. Find the large seam of fat where the bone was, on the left-hand side.

33 With your knife, cut along the seam to make two separate joints. Trim any sinews or tendon.

34 Next, remove the shoulder joints from the fore-end. With the ribs nearest you, and the thin shank in one hand, cut down the side of the ribs opposite the shank. Let the ribs guide your knife.

35 When you're halfway along, turn the joint around and carry on cutting along and down to the spine, with the neck end nearest you now.

36 When you hit the flat part of the spine, cut back towards yourself, rib end still closest to you. Keep cutting along until the shoulder falls away.

37 Cut away and discard the large seam of gristle running the length of the joint. Repeat the process with the other shoulder.

38 To bone out the shoulder, remove the knuckle by cutting through the joint and reserve this.

39 With the cut surface uppermost, simply feel for the short straight bone, (the humerus bone) and cut down its shank.

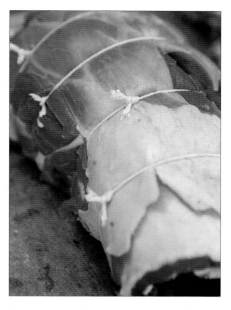

40 With the socket facing away from you, feeling along the bone with your fingers, ensure that the ridged side of the blade is on the board and the flat side is facing up. Cut down to meet the shoulder blade and, using scraping, sweeping strokes, cut around the flat faces of the blade bone.

41 Turning the joint over will help you bring the knife over the ridge of the shoulder blade.

▼ *Although these joints have been rolled for cooking whole, the cuts can also be diced or minced (ground), perhaps for a ragù with red wine, garlic and tomatoes.*

▲ *If a joint such as a whole shoulder has little natural fat, you can stud the meat with slivers of pork back fat.*

▲ *Leaving the bone in will give a more succulent roast and more juices for making the gravy.*

Tips for Cooking Large Deer
• When dicing venison for longer, slower cooking methods such as casseroling or braising, cut your dice a little larger than you would for beef, as venison does tend to shrink a little when cooking.
• Coating the venison dice in a really good dusting of well-seasoned flour before browning the pieces will help to thicken the sauce slightly. Fry the pieces a few at a time to ensure the pan is not crowded, otherwise the meat will stew in the oil rather than browning.
• Instead of the red wine suggested in many recipes, try ales, stouts and fruit juices for a refreshing change.

There's nothing better than fresh garden herbs and the subtle use of spices such as cloves, cinnamon, nutmeg, cardamom and star anise.
• If the hunter's breakfast perk doesn't appeal, try using the liver in a pâté. It's easy to substitute in most recipes for pork or chicken liver pâtés.

Camp-fire Hot Rock Venison Liver

After a kill it is always preferable to gut an animal as soon as possible, removing the organs. These deteriorate rapidly so they are best eaten first. In many hunting traditions across the world the eating of an animal's vital organs, especially the liver, is symbolic and, in some cases, ritualistic. In ancient times it was thought to give strength and courage to the hunter-warrior and was also often given as an offering of thanks to the gods for allowing the animal to be killed for food. This is an incredibly simple recipe, for which you don't even need a pan.

Serves 1

2 slices of venison liver about
    5mm/¼in thick, cut across its length
    (225–275g/8–10oz)
olive oil
sea salt and ground black pepper
1 tart eating apple, thinly sliced, and
    crusty bread, to serve

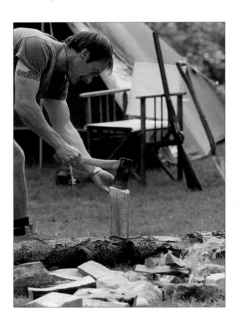

1 First prepare your fire and enough fuel to keep it going fiercely for at least half an hour.

2 You will also need to find a stone no less than 20–30cm/8–12in square and about 10–12cm/4–5in deep, with a relatively flat surface. If possible, avoid flint or layered stone such as slate, as these can splinter when heated.

Cook's tip If you have been driving in a very hot part of the world, you can try this cooking method on the super-hot bonnet of your vehicle. Use aluminium foil so that the meat does not come in direct contact with the metal.

3 Oil the top of the stone, then place it on the hottest area of the fire for 20–30 minutes until the top of the stone is hot. Test the heat of the surface by flicking water on to it; if the water spits and bubbles, the stone is hot enough.

4 While you are waiting for the stone to heat up, rub some olive oil over the liver.

5 Season the liver on both sides with plenty of salt and pepper.

6 Place the liver slices on the hot rock – they should sizzle immediately, and cook for 1–1½ minutes.

7 When the underside has browned, turn the slices over and cook the other side for 1 minute more. Remove the liver to a plate and leave to rest for a couple of minutes before eating with the apple slices and some crusty bread.

Energy 425kcal/1773kJ; Protein 42.2g; Carbohydrate 4.4g, of which sugars 0g; Fat 26.6g, of which saturates 7.3g; Cholesterol 540mg; Calcium 12mg; Fibre 0g; Sodium 162mg

Venison Cooked Under the Fire

Cooking under a fire is not only a slow method of cooking, it also takes a while to prepare the fire pit, so start early and make sure you have at least 6 hours' cooking time. Alternatively, if safe to do so, you can leave the meat cooking overnight, and wake up in the morning to a fabulous breakfast.

Serves 4–6

1 leg, haunch or shoulder from a
    small deer
1 orange, sliced
2 rosemary or thyme sprigs
150ml/¼ pint/⅔ cup red wine (or beer
    or water)
sea salt and ground black pepper
crusty rolls or bread, butter and
    cranberry sauce, to serve

1 Dig a hole at least 80cm/31in square and 20cm/8in deep. Line the hole with fresh, green foliage.

2 Stand some large flat rocks around the side of the pit, then add a layer of smaller rocks on top of the foliage. These will help to distribute the heat around the venison evenly.

3 On top of the layer of rocks add a couple of good handfuls of hay in the pit. This shouldn't be too dry, so dampen it before or after you place in the pit. Spread out evenly.

4 Take a double thickness of foil big enough to surround your joint, place the orange and herbs in the centre, season the meat well and place it on top.

5 Draw up the edges and sides of the foil and pour in the wine or beer, then twist and scrunch the foil to seal the package tightly. Use another double piece of foil to repeat the wrapping process; then repeat for a third time.

6 Place the venison in the centre of the pit and cover it with more fresh green foliage. Cover the pit with soil to a thickness of 2.5cm/1in and pat flat.

7 Arrange some large logs around the edge of the pit, and build the fire within.

8 Light the fire and keep it well stoked, topping it up continuously for 3 hours so there is a thick pile of hot embers before allowing the fire to die down.

9 At least another 3 hours later, or the next morning, remove the venison from the pit. The soil will still be hot so use a spade, then a cloth to gently dig out around the foil package. Be cautious of hot steam when opening the package.

10 The meat will strip easily from the bone and shred. Fill crusty rolls or slices of buttered bread with the meat and serve with cranberry sauce.

Energy 275kcal/1163kJ; Protein 55.6g; Carbohydrate 0.1g, of which sugars 0.1g; Fat 5.5g, of which saturates 2g; Cholesterol 125mg; Calcium 14mg; Fibre 0g; Sodium 140mg

Venison Kebab on the Barbecue

This recipe uses loin of venison, the most tender cut, which is suited to quick cooking and is preferably left pink to avoid drying out. The marinade can be made in advance and transported in a jar; it is suitable for most types of game so it is always worth taking on a hunting or fishing trip.
A barbecue is the best way to cook the kebab – remember to light it before preparing the kebab.
You will also need metal skewers, some thin sticks stripped of bark or some sturdy rosemary sprigs.

Serves 2

425g/15oz venison loin
1 medium red onion, peeled and cut
  into 8 even chunks
1 green (bell) pepper, cut into 8
  even chunks
2 tomatoes and 2 tortilla wraps or
  flatbreads, to serve

For the marinade
5ml/1 tsp cumin seeds, lightly toasted
  and crushed
5ml/1 tsp fennel seeds, lightly toasted
  and crushed
5ml/1 tsp sweet smoked paprika
1.5ml/¼ tsp dried chilli flakes
15ml/1 tbsp olive oil
sea salt

Variations Wild boar loin, wild goat loin, pigeon breast or duck breast can also be cooked in this way. In addition to the tomatoes, shredded lettuce and garlic mayonnaise would complete a very satisfying kebab.

1 Make the marinade by crushing the cumin and fennel seeds in a mortar and pestle. Transfer to a jar with a tight-fitting lid. Add the paprika, chilli flakes and oil, and shake. You can prepare this in advance at home.

2 Once the venison is boned, you will need to trim it. Remove the outer sinew by inserting the tip of a knife under the layer of sinew and cutting away from yourself. Draw the blade lengthways along the loin, tilting the blade slightly upwards into the sinew. Cut the loin into even-sized chunks.

3 Place the trimmed venison pieces in a plastic bag, pour in the marinade and massage the two together through the bag. Set aside for a minimum of 20 minutes, or until the fire is ready.

4 When the coals or embers are glowing and the flames have died down, take a skewer or clean stick, push a piece of venison on to the tip and slide it down the skewer. Follow with a segment of onion, then a piece of pepper, then another piece of meat.

5 Continue until there are equal pieces of meat and each vegetable on the skewer. Repeat with a second skewer.

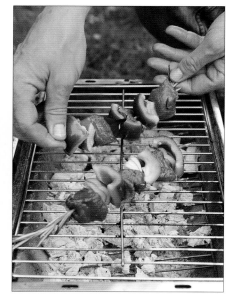

6 Season the kebabs with sea salt and place on the grill rack. Cook for 2 minutes before turning through 90 degrees and cooking for a further 2 minutes. Repeat this for each side before allowing the kebabs to rest at the side of the barbecue for 2 minutes.

7 Toast the flatbreads briefly on each side. Cut the tomatoes into chunks and season. Serve the kebabs with the warmed bread and tomatoes.

Energy 350kcal/1472kJ; Protein 50g; Carbohydrate 16.6g, of which sugars 14.1g; Fat 11g, of which saturates 2.7g; Cholesterol 106mg; Calcium 50mg; Fibre 3.8g; Sodium 133mg

Hunter's Venison Steak Baguette

This is a great snack that will quickly satisfy the hunger of a busy day in the field. A small hot fire and a heavy frying pan are all you need to cook it. This is a simple recipe that can be used for almost any of the tenderest cuts of game: try it with pigeon breast, or loin of boar.

Serves 1

225–275g/8–10oz steak 1.5cm/⅝in
   thick, taken from the top of the hind
   leg (effectively the rump), cutting
   directly towards the bone, across
   the grain
1 medium onion, peeled and
   thinly sliced
25g/1oz coarsely cracked
   black pepper
1 small baguette
10ml/2 tsp wholegrain mustard
15ml/1 tbsp mayonnaise
15ml/1 tbsp olive oil
sea salt and ground black pepper

1 Lay the steak on a flat surface and, with the back of a knife, tap it from one side to the other evenly and firmly enough to create ridges in the flesh.

2 Turn the meat through 90 degrees and repeat on the same side. Turn the steak over and repeat. This will help to tenderize the meat and will also help the pepper to adhere.

Variations This is the perfect hunter's lunch, and can be adapted to almost any type of game, so long as you use the tenderest cuts. A slice of wild boar rump or loin, duck breast, pigeon breast or hare and rabbit loin can be used instead of venison. You could also replace the mustard with a hot horseradish sauce, or if you're using birds, try cranberry sauce.

3 Sprinkle both sides of the steak with cracked black pepper, patting it on to the flesh to hold it in place. Put the steak to one side.

4 Heat the pan over a medium fire and add half of the olive oil. Fry the onions, stirring occasionally, until softened and beginning to brown.

5 When the onions are cooked, remove from the pan and set aside.

6 Return the pan to a hot part of the fire, so the heat is intense, and add the remaining oil. Let the oil heat until smoking hot.

7 Season the steak with sea salt and place in the pan.

8 Cook at a high temperature for 1½–2 minutes to give a good crust to the steak. Turn and cook for 1–1½ minutes more, then remove the pan from the heat and let the meat rest.

9 Split the baguette lengthways and spread the mustard over the two open surfaces; repeat with a layer of mayonnaise on each side.

10 Cut the steak across its length in 5mm/¼in slices and spread along the baguette. Finish by piling the fried onions on to the steak, close the sandwich and eat immediately.

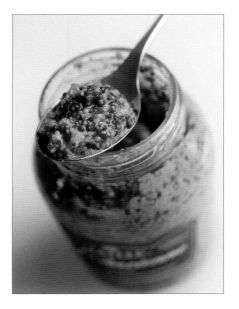

Energy 861kcal/3630kJ; Protein 65.2g; Carbohydrate 88.1g, of which sugars 6.4g; Fat 31.4g, of which saturates 5.9g; Cholesterol 124mg; Calcium 222mg; Fibre 3.1g; Sodium 1048mg

WILD BOAR & GOAT

Those who solely pursue boar and the various goat species often share an affinity with the hunters of deer – they delight in an altogether more organic, less contrived approach to shooting, where chance is celebrated. It matters little if your favoured quarry is the tricky Alpine chamois or a Latvian boar: for the hunter, there's little to rival the cathartic process of squeezing off that highly pressured shot to create something truly magical to eat. This chapter will take you from the high-adrenaline moment that your quarry drops to the relaxation and satisfaction of tending a camp fire, or pottering round a kitchen. It's this approach that is at the very core of the rifle shot: the quarry they connect with is honoured at the table.

◄ *Although goat and boar benefit from hanging and time for proper butchering, some cuts can be eaten at once, such as rump of boar, which is delicious cooked on hot coals.*

Preparing Wild Boar

Although a colossal male trophy boar may look very impressive, it'll be hard work to render him edible. Go for the younger animals if you have a choice. The ideal age and size for a boar is around 12–16 months, weighing 25–50kg/55–110lb.

The peripatetic lifestyle of truly wild boar keeps them very lean, and as they will eat literally anything – from fruit and flowers to acorns and carrion – their meat develops a huge range of flavours. A simple chop will hold a depth of taste that has been lost in domestically bred pork, yet its robustness can also handle strong flavour combinations. The only slight drawback with wild boar is that once you've tried it, domestic roast pork may never quite measure up to its wilder and fuller-flavoured cousin.

Unlike pork, the skin from truly wild boar is often too thick and hairy to be cooked and allowed to crisp, so most boar should be skinned before cooking. The exceptions are some feral pigs and boar crossbreeds, whose meat is a little closer to domestic pork.

Wild boar should always be cooked thoroughly to eliminate any chance of infection by *Trichinella* (roundworms).

▲ *The strong hearty flavour of wild boar is often used in the Hungarian dish pörkölt, flavoured with garlic, peppers and paprika. If the offal is in good condition it can lend an even earthier, more robust flavour and texture to this tasty and truly rustic peasant dish.*

Tips for Cooking Wild Boar
• Remember the difference between mature wild boar and a young animal, and adjust your cooking techniques accordingly. Mature wild boar demands a five-day marinade in plenty of good oil and an assortment of herbs.
• When considering the marinade, go for earthy herbs that you'd find in a cottage garden, such as sage, rosemary, tarragon and bay.
• Be wary of long exposure to wine marinades with young meat, owing to its propensity to turn purple if left for too long. Overnight is enough.
• Truly wild boar is not dissimilar to venison, so it's worth exploring tried and tested venison pairings such as sauces made with crushed juniper berries or dark (bittersweet) chocolate, as well as traditional pork recipes.
• When roasting a joint of young wild boar, either loin or leg, beware of its tendency to dry out: frequent basting is a must. Alternatively, lard the joint with bacon fat and then cover it with bacon or cured ham.

GUTTING A BOAR

1 To begin, make a small slit with your knife between the boar's foot and the hock joint on both hind legs. The hole should be made in the gap between the bone and the ligament. Insert a gambrel or other device. Hang the boar at a height suitable for you to work.

2 Remove both lower hind legs by cutting through the ligaments connecting the joint and then breaking the lower leg to sever it. Taking a little of the weight of the animal in your non-cutting hand can help you to get your knife into the required notch.

3 Remove the lower foreleg by cutting through the first joint above the foot. Repeat the process with the other leg. Long gloves are worn during the gralloching sequence, which is widely considered best practice with boar, as it helps to reduce the spread of disease.

4 Holding the penis in one hand, cut around this and up to and around the scrotum. Remove the genitals from their location and lay them down near the tail.

5 Cut down either side of any ducts or pipes into the flesh and down to the pelvis. With your fingers, hook the flesh away from the stomach sac.

6 Cut down until you reach the breastbone, then high up into the throat. There is a distinct hairline that you can follow with your knife.

7 Now return to the tail end and cut down with your saw into the pelvis by 2.5cm/1in or so. This will allow the carcass to cool and reduce 'bone taint'. Be careful not to nick the bladder.

8 Don't forget that, unlike farmed animals, wild boar will not have been starved prior to slaughter and their intestines may be quite full. In these cases, it may be prudent to tie off the lower intestine before you sever it.

9 Standing behind the carcass, continue the cutting line you've made from the genitals to loop around the anus, cutting under the tail. The genitals and various tubes should be held in one hand.

10 Returning to the front, the stomach sac will fall forward and allow access to the lower end of the intestines.

11 Severing at the point indicated will allow the loose section to drop clear of the cavity, avoiding contamination from digested matter.

12 Returning to the pelvis again, carefully cut the connecting tissues under the bladder, making sure you do not nick the bladder or any of the tubing leading from it. Once released, push this through the gap you've created to join the other organs and the section of lower intestine.

13 The whole collection should then come away in one go, with a little help from your knife near the base of the tail.

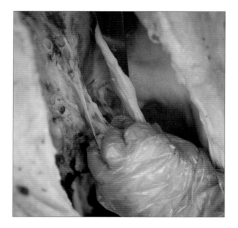

14 Investigate any lymph glands to ensure they are healthy. Look for any obvious irregularities, like discoloration or weeping.

15 Turning your attention to the breastbone now, run your saw down through the sternum.

16 You will now be able to remove the highest positioned kidney, located on the back wall of the cavity. The second kidney will be slightly lower down.

17 To free the lungs, heart and other organs in the chest area, carefully nick away the diaphragm from each side of the cavity walls.

18 Now cut down and beyond the larynx of the boar, then sever the windpipe and upper section of digestive tract as close to the tongue as possible.

19 Remove the head by cutting through the notch between the spine and the base of the skull. Pivoting the head will help you get the blade in the right place.

20 Check the cavity for fragments of ammunition and bone, paying particular attention to entry and exit wounds. Wipe away any blood.

Checking Internal Organs

Once the internal organs have been removed, inspect them for any signs of abnormality. If anything gives you cause for concern, the internal organs and the stomach should be bagged and labelled, and you should not eat any of the boar until you have sought advice from your local government agricultural health department. The carcass may have to be taken away and analysed in case there is some infection. If you feel the animal is in a generally poor state of health, it is best discarded as unfit for human consumption. Government agencies in many countries offer a test for Trichinosis/*Trichinella*.

• Check the lungs for grey patches, cysts or scar tissue.

• Lymph glands should be small and pale, not dark and enlarged. Look out for discharges.

• The liver should be a smooth gelatinous mass, without any hard areas, discoloration or lumps.

• The heart and kidneys should be free of scarring or anything unusual.

• Check with local agricultural and hunting bodies for advice on how to handle boar glands and offal.

SKINNING WILD BOAR

Boar, like domestic pigs, do need a degree of hanging time; if you are able to hang your boar in a cold store for over a week, so much the better. This will not only develop flavour and 'set' the animal's fat, it will also facilitate easier butchery and indeed skinning.

Skinning is important for boar, as the skin is so very tough. The ideal of wonderful, bubbly and blistered crackling is sadly not always achievable with truly wild boar.

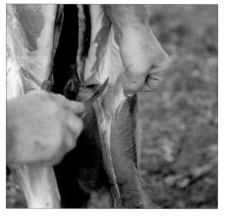

1 Suspend the boar at a comfortable height, and begin with the hind legs. Run the knife up from the middle of the boar's thigh to the hock joint and just past it. Avoid cutting the tendon.

2 Use short nicking cuts to free the skin, around the thigh. Repeat this process with the second leg. Cut through the tail, but leave it attached to the skin.

3 With both hands, gradually work the skin away from the back of the legs, the flanks and around the tail area. Use your knife for trickier areas.

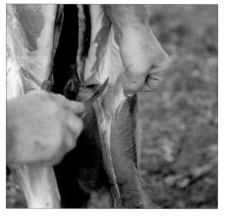

4 With both hands, or one hand and precise nicking cuts with your knife, work the skin gently away from the body, down towards the head.

5 Once you reach the shoulders and forelegs, you'll have to use your knife to carefully cut around this rather more complex area.

6 To remove the skin from the foreleg, run your knife tip from the severed joint up to meet the skinned shoulder area.

7 Then skin the second front leg in the same way.

8 Free any remaining skin from around the neck.

9 Split the carcass in half by sawing through it from the pelvis downward.

WILD BOAR BUTCHERY

1 To remove a hind leg, make a cut with your knife a finger's width from the aitch bone.

2 Cut at a perfect right angle to the spine. Saw through the bone, square to this initial cut, and finish with the knife.

3 Remove the tip of the tail bone; to make carving easier you can also remove the aitch bone.

4 Also for ease of carving, remove the halved section of pelvis by cutting along the flat side of this bone.

5 Keeping the cut side of the bone nearest to you, edge your knife along the bone towards the ball at the top of the femur, eventually exposing it.

6 Once the ball is detached from the socket, continue to follow the bone to the end, using short scraping strokes of the knife.

7 On the flat side of the pelvic bone, but under the socket, continue the same line to free the bone. Remove sinews, tendons and the lymph gland.

8 To remove the shank or knuckle, saw through the joint, or, as here, partially 'knuckle' the joint for roasting.

9 To remove the fore-end, count four ribs in from the neck end. Score a mark here, then saw through, parallel to the cut you made to remove the leg.

10 On the remaining loin section, remove the blade bone using small nicking cuts with your knife.

11 To remove the rib section from the shoulder, hold the rib part in your left hand and with small nicking cuts, cut along the rack of ribs.

12 Allow the meat to fall away as you cut along the side of the ribs. Remove any lymph glands. Next, you need to remove the 'spare-rib' from the 'hand'.

13 Locate the ball and socket joint between the humerus and blade bones. Cut straight down through this line, to separate the ball from the socket.

14 To remove the 'hand' – with this to the right and the shoulder to the left – keep the blade upright and try to pull it towards you as you separate the joints.

15 Here is the shoulder joint with the hand joint removed. The socket of the shoulder will now be visible to you as a point of reference.

16 Remove the blade bone from the shoulder rib; with the socket facing you, the ridged side of the blade down, feel along the bone with your fingers.

17 Work the blade along the bone edges using very shallow strokes with the knife tip. Avoid cutting too deep and increasing the chance of wasting meat.

18 Turn the joint over to help the knife over the shoulder blade. Continue to work the blade along the bone edges to free the shoulder blade.

19 Cut down to meet the shoulder blade and use scraping, sweeping strokes to cut around the flat faces of the blade bone.

20 The boned shoulder is now ready to be rolled and strung. Joints look tidier once strung, keeps it together while cooking, and carving will be easier too.

21 Now turn your attention to the hand section. The hand is a versatile joint that roasts well, having one central bone which conducts heat.

22 Start on the knuckle by cutting through the joint to remove it from the hand. This has very little meat on it, but can be used for stock or gravy.

23 Cut straight down the length of the bone, and continue cutting to release the flesh on all sides. Trim out any lymph glands and silvery sinews.

24 Boning the hand will give you a fairly large bone to roast for stock. This is an easy bone to remove and will boost your confidence in butchery.

▲ *With the shoulder boned out and the humerus removed from the hand, the meat can be minced (ground) or diced.*

25 Now remove the belly from the loin. Begin with the ribs nearest you and cut through the lean part of the chump end.

26 Score a guide line parallel to the spine with your knife, then saw along this line through the ribs. Finish the cutting line with the knife.

27 If there is any loose or excess fat, pull this away. Keeping your hand flat on the ribs, run the length of the blade towards you, tight against the bones.

28 If you prefer, you may find it easier to stand the rack or rib section up to do this. Make sure the knife runs tightly down the ribs to free the belly meat.

29 The complete sheet of belly with the rack of ribs removed: the numerous recipes for slow-cooked belly pork really come into their own using boar.

30 To remove the short loin from the loin, locate the end of the chump bone by prodding with your knife tip. Make a mark with the knife at this point.

31 Then cut straight down with the knife until you reach bone, and finish this cut with your saw.

32 To cut steaks from the short loin, remove the chump bone by running the knife along its edge. Use short nicks until the bone can be removed.

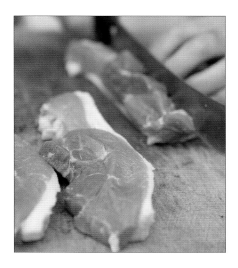

▲ With the chump bone removed, the short loin is easily carved into steaks.

33 Remove the spinal cord before cutting chops from the short loin. Do this by simply drawing it out with the help of your knife.

34 To take chops from the short loin, simply allow the ribs to guide your knife down to the bone. Finish each cut with a sharp blow from your cleaver.

Preparing Wild Goat

Without doubt, the younger the animal the better it will be to eat. Determining the age of any species of wild goat is not easy to do, but if you intend to cook what you've shot you have to accept the element of luck involved. A distinct lack of front incisors will confirm an aged goat of over five years.

Aged male goats will almost certainly have a very powerful musky odour to them – strong enough to permanently taint any clothing or room it comes into contact with, let alone the meat itself. A female goat will provide markedly less pungent meat.

Goat lends itself well to slow-cooked Mediterranean-style stews and casseroles, with robust and fragrant additions like tomatoes, garlic and herbs. Moist, tomato-based curries, with lots of gravy or sauce, also showcase goat meat wonderfully. If you've taken a youngish animal with a generous coating of fat, temper it with something sharp: zesty sauces made with citrus fruits or vinegar-based marinades.

▶ *Be careful of any splintered bones when gutting a shot animal.*

GUTTING A GOAT

1 To begin, make a small slit with your knife between the goat's foot and the hock joint on both hind legs. The hole should be made in the gap between the bone and the ligament. A cut of around 2.5cm/1in will allow the insertion of a gambrel or other device to allow the beast to be suspended by its hind legs.

2 At the tip of the goat's breastbone, make a small, shallow cut with your knife tip, large enough for you to insert a couple of fingers. Gently working your fingers in will loosen the skin away from the stomach sac. Puncturing the stomach sac is not pleasant, so be very careful with your knife.

3 With a carpet-fitter's knife fitted with a hooked blade, carefully slit the skin upwards towards the pelvis area – keeping your fingers hard against the stomach sac should protect it from being nicked by the blade. Do not rush this. If you do, much of the meat could be ruined.

4 The weight of the stomach will help it drop down and out through the slit you've made. Remember that a wild goat is likely to have a full digestive tract when it is shot, so there will be a considerable amount of matter in the gut. Make sure you avoid contaminating the flesh with this.

5 Run the tip of your knife around the animal's anus (and the opening of the organs if female) and pull this part up and proud of the body. Tie the openings off and secure very tightly with string or twine. This will prevent any contents seeping on to the meat as you pull this section through.

6 Returning to the cavity area, pull the digestive tract and uterus, if present, through the hole and allow these to sit on the stomach sac. Remove the kidneys. Wedging the cavity open with a prop will help the temperature of the carcass to drop more quickly and prevent spoilage, but this is optional.

7 Inspect the lymph glands for any irregularities, discoloration or weeping. Anything other than pristine lymph glands indicate a possible health issue.

8 To release the stomach sac, sever the gullet close to the breastbone. The stomach sac should fall to the ground.

9 Use a saw to cut down through the rigid breastbone. Splitting the pelvic bone at this point as well will allow the carcass to cool a little more quickly.

10 Trim out and discard the diaphragm, keeping your knife blade very close to the breastbone.

11 Release the pluck – the heart, lungs and liver – by cutting through the windpipe high into the throat.

12 Wipe out the cavity thoroughly with a clean cloth, removing as much blood as possible. Remove any visible debris.

SKINNING WILD GOAT

1 Run the knife, blade uppermost, from the middle of the goat's thigh up to the hock joint and stop there, or just past it. Using short, nicking cuts, cut around the joint. Avoid cutting the tendon.

2 Repeat this process with the second leg, working the skin away from the back of the legs, the flanks and around the tail area. Cut through the tail, leaving it attached to the skin.

3 With both hands, or gentle nicking cuts, work the skin gently away down towards the neck. The goat's age, fat content and temperature will affect how easily the skin is removed.

4 Once you reach the shoulders and forelegs, use your knife to cut around this slightly more complicated area.

5 Free any remaining skin from round the neck, then skin the second front leg. Cut just behind the ears at the natural gap in the joint to remove the head.

6 To remove the feet, find the notch on the joint and work your knife into the gap, cutting through the connective tissue.

WILD GOAT BUTCHERY

1 To remove the breasts, run the knife from the top of the thigh along the flank to the loin. Finish under the shoulder.

2 You will be able to cut through only half of this section with your knife. Finish with a saw, following the same line.

3 Repeat on the other side. Trim any loose tissue and sinew and remove any lymph glands from the exposed area.

4 Now separate the shoulders from the fore-end or quarter rib section: make a cut close to the shoulder section, between the sixth and seventh rib, then cut along the edge of the rib nearest the shoulder until you reach the spine.

5 Continue cutting through the rib meat on the opposite side. Cut through the spine with your saw. The fore quarter is now separated from the trunk.

6 To remove the shoulder from the ribcage, turn your knife slightly flatter and follow the ribs with the blade down towards the spine, keeping as close to the ribcage as you can to ensure you lose as little meat as possible.

7 Cut through the meaty portion of the neck at a right angle to the spine, until you reach the bone. Free the joint from the neck end of the spine by cutting along the spine towards you.

8 Finally, remove the large strip of yellow gristle running the length of the joint. This is an ideal time to check for bone splinters and any ammunition fragments.

9 Remove the lymph gland found between the neck and foreleg. Inspect each gland you remove. Bloated, discoloured or weeping lymph glands may indicate an animal not fit to eat.

10 Remove the haunches (hind legs) from the trunk: with your knife tip, probe the hip area until you feel the pelvis – not far from the spine. Mark this point.

11 Using this as a guide, cut across the body. Keep your knife at a right-angle to the spine. Any subsequent cuts across the spine should be parallel to this cut.

12 Change to a saw when you need to cut through the spine and revert to the knife to finish cutting the line. Brush and wipe away any bone fragments.

13 Use your knife on the same parallel through the line on the flank opposite. Wipe away any bone fragments.

14 To divide the legs, with the pelvis nearest you, cut through the groin until you feel the pelvis, then saw through the spine. Continue through the flesh with your knife to separate the two legs.

15 To remove a shank from a leg, find the gap in the knee joint indicated here and make a mark with your knife there. This may take a few attempts. Cut through the leg at this point.

16 Now remove the loin from the haunches. Locate the gap at the end of the pelvic bone and cut through the line of the flank untill you reach the spine.

17 Now, cut smartly right through the spine with your saw.

18 To bone out the shoulder, start with the joint skin-side down and remove the knuckle by cutting through the joint. Reserve the knuckle for gravy or stock.

19 Find the seam between the neck fillet and shoulder with the knife tip. Cut along to remove the fillet in one piece.

20 Having removed the fillet, you'll be left with the section containing the humerus and the blade bone.

21 Separate the blade bone from the humerus by cutting through the connective tissue within the socket.

22 Keeping the cut surface uppermost, feel for the short bone, and cut down the shaft. Keep cutting until the bone is freed and can be removed.

23 To remove the blade bone, feel for the bone with your fingers (flat side face up) and cut down to the shoulder blade. Scrape round the flat sides of the bone.

24 Turning the joint over will help you bring the knife over the ridge of the shoulder blade. The boned-out shoulder joint is now ready for dicing.

▲ *From top: the removed knuckle, humerus and blade bones.*

25 Next, bone out the loin: begin with the loin skin side down, making a cut on one side of the spine.

26 Continue to work your knife tip down all faces of the spine, being careful not to cut through the skin at all, until it can be removed from the joint.

27 Not cutting through the skin ensures the loin is kept as a single, pristine, rectangular sheet of meat. This is ideal for stuffing and rolling.

28 To cut the chump end from the rump, start with the femur head facing up and to the left as you look down at it. Cut down at this point.

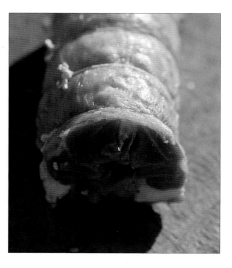

▲ *The loin, boned, rolled and strung, is ideal for a pot roast.*

29 To make chops from the loin, first remove the rib section from it. Use the saw to cut through the spine.

30 Now split the spine down the middle vertically, beginning at the opposite end to the ribs. You will need to use a saw or a cleaver for this job.

31 Using the ribs to guide you, cut down through the flesh to the bone. Finish the cuts with a cleaver if your knife is not heavy enough.

▲ These little cutlets can be cooked in moments over hot coals. A lime and chilli marinade or jerk rub works well.

32 Now remove the halved section of pelvis, or aitch bone, from a haunch by cutting along the flat side of the pelvis.

33 Keeping the cut side of the bone nearest you, edge your knife along the bone towards the ball of the femur.

34 You'll eventually expose the head of the femur. Once you've cut around the ball of the joint and separated it from the socket, continue with short scraping strokes to the end of the bone.

35 Again, working on the flat side of the pelvic bone, but this time under the socket, continue the same line as before to free the bone.

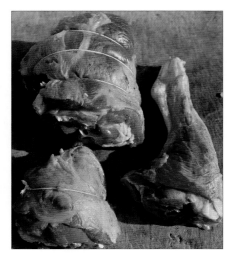

▲ The rolled leg (top), chump and hock removed; the hock or shank (right) and the chump (bottom), boned and rolled.

Preparing Wild Kid

If you've had to take a very young wild goat, or a kid as a follower at foot, you can be sure that the meat will be young enough to be perfect for roasts and the faster cooking methods like frying and grilling. Kid has its own unique flavour, somewhere midway between veal and lamb, but it can be treated like lamb if you're struggling for ideas. The texture of kid and lamb is very similar, although generally lamb would have a slightly higher fat content.

As a rough guide to aging a goat, a newborn kid has four pairs of milk teeth at the front of its mouth for its first year. After a year, it loses one pair to a pair of adult incisors. By the age of two, it has two pairs of incisors and by the time it reaches four it will probably have a full set of eight adult teeth.

▶ *To gut a kid, start by suspending it using a gambrel, following the instructions given for wild goat.*

GUTTING A KID

1 Locate the tip of the breastbone and make a small hole with your knife tip. Gently work two fingers in to separate the hide from the stomach sac.

2 Using a carpet-fitter's knife fitted with a curved blade, slit the skin upwards towards the pelvis – keep your fingers pressed against the stomach sac to prevent it being punctured by the blade.

3 The goat's gut will fall down and out through the cavity you've made. Remember that there will be a lot of food matter in the animal's gut and digestive tracts.

4 Run the tip of your knife around the anus, pull this flesh up and away from the body and secure tightly with string or twine to prevent any matter seeping on to and spoiling the meat.

5 Returning to the cavity area, pull the colon and uterus, if the animal is female, through the hole made with your knife and allow these to rest on the stomach sac. Remove both kidneys.

6 Sever the gullet close to the breastbone. The stomach sac should now fall to the ground. With a younger animal, you can continue to cut down through the breastbone with a knife.

7 Propping open the cavity with a stick will help it to cool more quickly and prevent spoilage. Trim out the diaphragm, keeping your knife blade as close to the breastbone as possible.

8 The pluck – the heart, lungs and liver – will all fall away into your hand. Release these organs by cutting through the windpipe as high into the throat area as possible.

9 To remove the head, cut through just behind the ears, feeling for the natural gap in the joint. Splitting down through the pelvic bone allows the carcass to cool a little more quickly.

SKINNING A KID

1 Run the knife, blade uppermost, from the middle of the goat's thigh up to the hock joint and stop there or just past it. Using short, nicking cuts, cut around the joint, avoiding the tendon at all costs.

2 Repeat this process with the second leg, working the skin away from the back of the legs and around the tail area. Cut through the tail, leaving it attached to the skin.

3 With both hands, or nicking cuts with your knife, work the skin gently away from the body towards the neck. The fat content and temperature will affect how easily the skin is removed.

4 Once you reach the shoulders, you'll have to use your knife instead of your hands to pick around this rather more difficult area.

5 To remove the skin from the foreleg, run your knife tip from the first joint closest to the hoof up to meet the skinned shoulder area.

6 Gently free any remaining skin from around the neck and then skin the second front leg as before.

PREPARING KID FOR GRILLING WHOLE

1 A kid is small enough to cook whole, either 'spatchcocked' on the grill, or for a spit roast. Firstly, if you haven't already removed the hooves in the field, remove all four now; find the notch on the joint closest to the foot and work your knife into this tight gap, cutting through the connective tissue.

2 Then simply break the joint with your hands. Repeat this with the other three hooves and discard them.

3 ▶ With the kid on its back and its neck nearest you, saw down either side of the backbone, using long, even strokes, all the way along, beginning at the pelvis.

4 Do not saw all the way though the bones – just around halfway. You may wish to approach the goat from the tail end halfway through this process.

5 Weakening the rigidity of the spine in this way makes it much easier to keep the kid flat. This will ensure that it cooks far more evenly.

6 Bend and push the hind legs as far as they will naturally go at the knee and forcibly fold the thigh flat across the pelvis; this will help keep the legs flat.

Tips for Cooking Wild Kid
• If the kid is young enough, the faster cooking methods will work. Don't be afraid to barbecue or grill cutlets – just remember to brush or baste them well.

• North African tagine recipes are well suited to kid or goat. They are full of spicy flavours, not necessarily hot, and are usually balanced with fruit such as apricots, preserved lemons or prunes.

• Caribbean flavours and recipes also work superbly with kid. Curried goat is worth trying: the authentic Jamaican blend of spices includes cayenne, cumin, cardamom, coriander, turmeric and chilli.

Boar and Rosemary Kebabs

For this recipe you will need two sturdy stems of rosemary. You might find a bush growing where you happen to be, but in case you don't, take with you some stout lengths of rosemary to use as skewers. The boar is doused in lemon juice and left to marinate, which helps to tenderize the meat.

Serves 1

2 x 20cm/8in rosemary stems
275–350g/10–12oz rump of boar,
   cut into strips
1 lemon
10ml/2 tsp olive oil
1 large red (bell) pepper
handful of shredded lettuce
sea salt and ground black pepper
flatbreads, to serve

1 Strip the rosemary leaves from the stems and reserve. Take one of the rosemary twigs and with the thinner end, pierce a strip of meat 1cm/½in from its end, pushing the meat while turning the sprig to penetrate.

2 Fold the meat in half and push the point through the other end to form a crescent shape. Repeat this action to fill the skewer with half the strips, then skewer the remaining meat on the other rosemary stem.

3 Place the skewers on a tray or in a plastic bag and squeeze over the lemon juice. Tear the reserved rosemary leaves and scatter these over too. Rub the lemon juice and rosemary into the meat with your fingers.

4 Meanwhile, prepare a barbecue and when the coals are hot, lay the pepper on the grill rack and allow the skin to blacken, turning the pepper until it is charred all over. Place in a plastic bag and seal. Leave to cool.

Variation You could also try this recipe with venison or goat.

5 Brush the rosemary off the meat (to prevent it burning), season the kebabs with salt and pepper and drizzle the oil over the meat.

6 Place on the grill rack and cook for 2 minutes. Turn and cook for a further 2 minutes, then check to see if the meat is cooked through. If any is still pink, return the kebabs to the heat for a further 2 minutes on each side.

7 Scrape the skin off the pepper, discard the seeds and tear the flesh into strips. Serve with the kebabs, shredded lettuce and warmed flatbreads.

Energy 459kcal/1923kJ; Protein 61.4g; Carbohydrate 12.9g, of which sugars 12.4g; Fat 18.2g, of which saturates 5g; Cholesterol 173mg; Calcium 61mg; Fibre 3.7g; Sodium 203mg

Fire-grilled Wild Boar Chop

A boar chop taken from the loin is a great cut to cook quickly outdoors, as it has a nice 'eye' of tender meat with a good layer of fat, and it sits on a bone to ensure a tasty result. A quick rub with aromatics and a traditional accompaniment of grilled polenta will turn the chop into a classic mountain dish, which can be cooked on a portable stove or over an open fire.

Serves 1

1 wild boar chop, 4cm/1½in thick
   (singe off any hairs over the fire)
5ml/1 tsp paprika
5ml/1 tsp dried oregano
1 garlic clove, crushed
15ml/1 tbsp olive oil
½ block of pre-cooked polenta, cut
   into 3 slices (see Cook's tip)
juice of ½ lemon
sea salt and ground black pepper

1 First marinate the chop – this can be done inside a plastic bag to avoid too much handling. Place the chop in the bag with the paprika, oregano, garlic and 5ml/1 tsp of the oil, seal and massage the aromatics into the meat. Set aside for at least 20 minutes.

2 Heat a frying pan over the fire. Add 5ml/1 tsp of the oil, and heat.

3 Remove the chop from the bag and season with salt and pepper; lay it in the hot oil and seal one side over high heat for 1½–2 minutes then turn for a further 1½–2 minutes to seal the other side.

4 Move the pan to a cooler part of the fire, or push the embers away so the heat is less intense. Flip the chop to the original side and cook for 4–6 minutes, moving the meat around the pan occasionally. Turn on to the second side for another 4–6 minutes, again moving the chop occasionally.

Cook's tip Make the polenta the day before. Bring 300ml/½ pint/1¼ cups water to the boil in a small, heavy pan with a pinch of salt. Pour in 75g/3oz/ ¾ cup quick-cook polenta, whisking as you do so, then reduce the heat to low and cook for 7–8 minutes, stirring constantly with a wooden spoon, until thick. Scrape out into a container and refrigerate. When the polenta has set firm it can be sliced.

5 Remove the meat from the pan to rest. Move the pan to a hotter area of the fire, add the remaining oil and the polenta slices, and cook for 5 minutes on each side, until the polenta is crisp and golden.

6 Return the chop to the pan to reheat for 30 seconds on each side, along with any juices that have collected. When the meat is sizzling again, squeeze in the lemon juice and then return the polenta to the pan to soak up the lemony meat juices. Serve immediately.

Energy 639kcal/2675kJ; Protein 52.2g; Carbohydrate 73.1g, of which sugars 0g; Fat 14.3g, of which saturates 3.2g; Cholesterol 126mg; Calcium 17mg; Fibre 2.2g; Sodium 140mg

Greek Island Grilled Kid

Kid has been cooked to celebrate religious festivals across the world for hundreds of years, especially on the islands of Greece. A favourite at Easter time, a whole kid may be spit-roasted to ensure there is plenty to serve the family gathered for the festivities. Here the kid is spatchcocked so that it can be laid flat on a makeshift barbecue built on the ground. If you build this so that you can adjust the height of the grill, you will have better control over the cooking. Ordinarily eaten with a selection of salads, vegetables and breads, the kid is served here with a composite salad of potato, fennel, feta and olive.

Serves 8–10

1 kid (weighing 7–8kg/15–17½ lb)
    skinned, gutted and cleaned
sea salt and ground black pepper

For the baste
grated rind and juice of 3 lemons
1 bunch oregano, roughly chopped
1 bunch thyme, roughly chopped
1 bunch dill, roughly chopped
8 garlic cloves, peeled and crushed
30ml/2 tbsp fennel seeds, crushed
275ml/9fl oz/1 generous cup light
    olive oil

For the salad
2.75kg/6lb new potatoes, scrubbed
    and cut into large dice
2 plump fennel heads, stems removed,
    each cut into 8 wedges
grated rind and juice of 2 lemons
250ml/8fl oz/1 cup extra virgin olive oil
200g/7oz feta cheese
40 black or kalamata olives, pitted
2 large handfuls flat leaf parsley,
    coarsely chopped
sea salt and ground black pepper

1 To make the baste, put the lemon rind and juice, herbs, garlic, fennel and oil in a jar, shake vigorously and leave to infuse (steep) for at least 1 hour. When you are ready to cook, shake again and rub some baste into both sides of the kid.

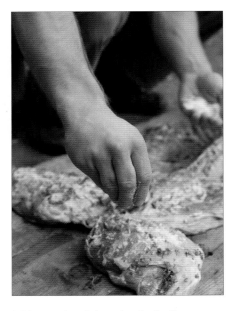

2 Next, rub salt into the flesh. If you have time, leave the kid to marinate for up to 1 hour while you build and light the barbecue. You can use wood as well as charcoal on the fire if you prefer, to add an authentic smoky taste.

3 When the flames have died down and you have a bed of hot embers, transfer the kid to the grill. You may want to use foil to protect the meat from the fierce heat. Baste every so often.

4 The loin and saddle will cook much more quickly than the limbs, so once the flesh begins to brown, move the grill up to its higher setting where the heat is less intense. Turn the kid over after about 1–1½ hours. It should be cooked after 4 hours but do not hurry it – wait until the meat comes away easily from the bone.

5 To make the salad, put the potatoes into a large pan of boiling salted water and simmer gently for 8–10 minutes, drain and allow to steam dry.

6 Place the fennel, lemon rind and juice, olive oil and some seasoning in a pan, cover and bring to a simmer. Cook gently for 5 minutes then transfer the fennel to a large bowl. Add the still warm potatoes and toss them together.

7 When the kid is ready to serve, crumble the feta into the salad bowl, add the olives and parsley and mix.

8 Remove the kid from the fire and place it on a large board, or a large piece of foil on the ground. The best way to eat this is for everyone to sit around it and pull the tender meat away from the bones with their fingers. Alternatively, you may want to carve the meat yourself, pile it on to a large platter, and serve it with the salad.

Energy 1190kcal/4928kJ; Protein 28g; Carbohydrate 44.9g, of which sugars 4.2g; Fat 102.7g, of which saturates 45.1g; Cholesterol 152mg; Calcium 113mg; Fibre 3.5g; Sodium 600mg

Outdoor Wild Goat Pipérade

Pipérade originated in the Basque region of France and is commonly eaten for breakfast. Adding meat turns it into a filling lunch or supper, and the flavour of goat suits the sweet taste of the peppers. This one-pot meal is ideal for cooking in the field.

Serves 4–6

30ml/2 tbsp olive oil
2 large onions, thinly sliced
1kg/2¼lb goat thigh, cut into
    2cm/¾in pieces
4 bushy thyme sprigs
300ml/½ pint/1¼ cups white wine
5ml/1 tsp sweet smoked paprika
1 red (bell) pepper, sliced
1 green (bell) pepper, sliced
2 garlic cloves, sliced
250g/9oz ripe tomatoes, sliced
5 eggs
10 basil leaves, torn
sea salt and ground black pepper

3 When the meat is tender add the paprika, peppers, garlic and tomatoes and season. Cover and simmer gently for 15 minutes, stirring occasionally.

1 Warm a pan on the fire and add the oil and onions. Season the goat and add it to the pan. Fry for 4–5 minutes or until the goat is browned.

4 When the peppers are soft, whisk the eggs and add the basil. Pour into the pot and stir to scramble the eggs, then serve immediately.

2 Add the thyme and wine and bring to the boil. Move the pan to a cooler part of the fire, cover and cook slowly for 1–1¼ hours, stirring occasionally.

Energy 473kcal/1971kJ; Protein 39.5g; Carbohydrate 10.1g, of which sugars 8.4g; Fat 27.4g, of which saturates 10.6g; Cholesterol 285mg; Calcium 65mg; Fibre 2.2g; Sodium 211mg

Cutlets of Wild Goat on the Barbecue

Wild goat is a hard-working creature, often grazing on rocky outcrops with little fodder. Although tasty, the meat can often be tough, but the cutlets are still good for grilling even if they do need a little extra attention. These cutlets are to be cooked on the barbecue so you will need to prepare this.

Serves 4

16 goat cutlets, trimmed
30ml/2 tbsp natural (plain) yogurt
15ml/1 tbsp mint leaves, chopped
4 thick slices rustic bread
1 garlic clove, halved
sea salt and ground black pepper
tomato, red onion and olive salad,
   to serve

1 Place the cutlets in a plastic bag and spoon the yogurt on top. Add the mint leaves and season with plenty of salt and pepper.

2 Seal the bag and massage the contents so that all the cutlets are covered in the yogurt on both sides. Set aside to marinate for 20–30 minutes, longer if possible, as this will help make the meat tender.

3 Remove the cutlets from the bag and scrape off the excess yogurt.

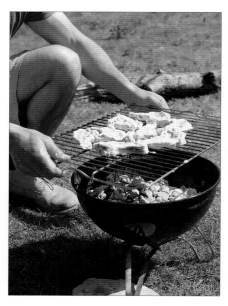

4 When the coals are ready, arrange the cutlets on the grill rack, and place on the barbecue. Cook gently over medium heat so as not to rush the cooking.

5 Allow 4 minutes on each side, then turn and cook for 2 more minutes on each side. When the cutlets are nearly done, place thick slices of rustic bread on the barbecue and toast lightly.

6 Rest the cutlets on the edge of the barbecue for 5 minutes before serving.

Variation The yogurt and mint marinade can be used for venison chops and wild boar chops as well as goat; the cooking times will vary depending on the thickness of the cutlets.

7 While the cutlets are resting, remove the toast from the grill and drizzle with olive oil. Rub the toast with a cut clove of fresh garlic.

8 Serve the cutlets and toast alongside a chunky mixed salad of tomato, red onion, olives and mint dressed with lemon juice and olive oil.

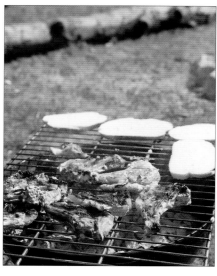

Energy 596kcal/2503kJ; Protein 62.7g; Carbohydrate 30.3g, of which sugars 2.4g; Fat 25.8g, of which saturates 12.1g; Cholesterol 220mg; Calcium 93mg; Fibre 2g; Sodium 418mg

RABBIT, HARE & SQUIRREL

The rough shooter is unencumbered by etiquette requirements, any kind of dress code and the inevitable tips of fellow guns. With fewer expectations and considerably less financial outlay, the only concerns are personal safety, nature's own slideshow and what the spoils will be. The shooter will delight at whatever a hedgerow or a field of sugar beet may conjure up. Similarly, the silent pigeon shooter, hardly moving, squinting up as the first few pigeons of dusk come floating into the treetops, won't fail to grab the opportunity of a squirrel scuttling towards a drey or the first rabbits appearing for their evening graze. These creatures, regarded as pests for the havoc they wreak on farm and woodland, will make some of the tastiest dishes you could possibly wish for.

◄ *Paella is traditionally cooked outside, with rabbit as a favourite ingredient, and this is the perfect camp fire recipe.*

Preparing Rabbit

The humble rabbit is a sustainable staple for rough shooters throughout the world. It is remarkably versatile and can be cooked in many ways – most chicken recipes will work with rabbit. A rabbit aged around three to four months offers a good meat yield but still has the perfect succulence only a truly youthful animal can offer.

Immediately after dispatch, a rabbit should have its bladder emptied: running the flat side of your thumb from the sternum to the rabbit's thigh should expel any urine in the bladder. Ideally, it should be paunched very quickly and cooked when fresh. There is little value in hanging rabbits.

If you're selecting a rabbit to cook, aim for soft, pliable ears and clean, sharp claws that have not yet been blunted with age. A young rabbit can be roasted whole, while older animals are better jointed and slow-cooked. If the rabbits in your area taste a little too strong, an overnight immersion in salted water will temper this flavour a little.

Tips for Cooking Rabbit

• Freezing rabbit can dry the meat out, so use it as fresh as possible.
• Any rabbit that has been killed with a shotgun and is destined for the table should be carefully examined for any bone fragments. Lead shot can splinter rabbit bones very easily.
• Rabbit meat marries very well with milder-flavoured shellfish, such as mussels and crayfish. Consider twinning them in risottos, frittatas and even pies.
• Hind legs can be boned out, as you would pheasant legs, and stuffed with pork or similar savoury stuffings. A mixture of pâté and fried mushrooms would make an extremely tasty stuffing.

▶ Rabbits will usually be gutted by the time they arrive in the kitchen, but if not you will need to paunch, or gut, them before they are skinned.

SKINNING A RABBIT

1 Unlike birds, rabbits are almost free of any smells and are quick to gut. Slit the stomach, just below the skin, from sternum to rectum. Remove the contents from the cavity, and insert a clean stick to hold the incision open. Remove the feet on both hind legs at the first joint. Cut the tendon with a knife as a cleaver may splinter the bone.

2 Flatten a leg and run the knife tip down from the hip socket (locate this by feeling with your fingers through the skin) to the first joint. Repeat this process with the other leg. Try to work the fur away from the clean exposed flesh to reduce the chances of any contamination of the meat.

3 Work the skin gently away from the hind legs and clear any remaining tufts of fur away from the meat, paying particular attention to the exposed knuckle area. Cut from the inside of the pelt outwards. With the hind feet removed, the skin should easily 'pop' over the lower part of the hind legs.

4 Holding both hind legs in one hand, work the pelt away towards the head.

5 Keep pulling the pelt towards the head until it is stripped back to the shoulders. The tail will probably have stayed attached to the rear end of the rabbit.

6 Cut away the tail using a knife. Then, using a cloth or a piece of kitchen paper to help you grip it, pull away the remaining section of the rabbit's rectum in one piece.

7 Carefully work the pelt over the shoulders, exposing the front legs or 'wings'. When enough of the neck is exposed, cut through the flesh with your knife, then cut the bone with a cleaver.

8 Cut down through the pelvis, finishing by leaning down on to the back of the blade. Clear away any remaining bone fragments or mess. The rabbit is now ready to cook whole.

JOINTING A RABBIT

1 To divide the rabbit into joints, start by removing the hind legs just below the loin section.

2 Then separate the legs with a single blow from a cleaver or heavy knife. Most recipes require just the larger hind legs from the rabbit, along with the loin.

3 Separate the loin from the rib section using a cleaver if need be. For fun you can prepare a 'rack' of rabbit as an appetizer: fiddly but impressive.

Preparing Hare

Sadly, the hare rarely receives the recognition it thoroughly deserves. If treated carefully, hare can provide an array of luxurious dishes with a unique flavour and succulence. There is little difficulty in slow-cooking a hare, provided it has been jointed and marinated well in something tenderizing and flavoursome, but roasting hare successfully is a little trickier.

To begin with, you really need a youthful animal, ideally in its first year. Look for soft, silky ears and milky-white teeth – the teeth yellow with age. The coat should be fairly soft and smooth too; it shouldn't be too coarse, grey and wiry. Older animals also have a far more pronounced harelip and sport a little greyness around the nose and mouth. Small, sharp claws are a good sign of youth, as the claws grow longer and blunt with age.

There is more than enough flavour in a hare without hanging it for a week, unless you like it particularly 'high'. One day, two at the most, is enough – head down and with the insides still in place, somewhere cool and free of flies.

▶ *The depth of gamey flavour puts many people off eating hare but, as with any other game animal or bird, the flavour depends on the the length of hanging time and the skill of the cook.*

Tips for Cooking Hare

• When you are collecting the blood from a hare, adding a little red wine vinegar to the receptacle will stop the blood coagulating before use.
• If for any reason you don't have the hare's blood to thicken the final dish, whisk a little beurre manié (some flour and softened unsalted butter worked into a paste) into your simmering stock or sauce.
• Avoid using heavy beef stocks when making hare dishes as they tend to destroy any subtle flavours; chicken, vegetable or even a light lamb stock is preferable.
• The meat from a hare, slow-cooked in red wine, garlic, basil and oregano and then forked away from the bones, makes a superb basis for a rich ragù to serve with your favourite pasta.
• Using caul fat from a pig is an ideal way to keep a roasted hare moist throughout cooking. Caul fat membranes can be obtained from good butchers and online suppliers.
• Hare that you suspect to be a little too gamey in flavour can be soaked overnight in a thin mixture of milk and water. This will calm any overbearing flavours.

1 With the hare hanging head down, cut into the skin just above the sternum and slide the blade up to the base of the stomach cavity.

2 Pull down and remove the contents of the cavity, leaving the kidneys either side of the spine and the heart, liver and lungs in the ribcage.

3 The blood will have collected inside the ribcage. If you wish to reserve it, tilt the shoulders and head up to allow the blood to run into a pot or jug (pitcher).

4 Cutting a little farther through the sternum down towards the throat can free up any remaining blood. Drain this off in the same way.

5 Prop open the freshly cleaned cavity with a clean stick to accelerate cooling. When you're ready to skin the hare, pull out the heart, liver and lungs.

6 With the hare on its back, run the tip of the knife from the middle part of the inner thigh down towards the foot. Repeat this process with the other leg.

7 Work the skin away from the legs completely using your thumbs; the skin should tear near to the feet, which will be removed later.

8 Holding the hind legs in one hand, pull the leg skin and the tail section down towards the head area. Release any slightly trickier areas with the knife.

9 With the head now enveloped by the skin, remove the head with a single blow from your cleaver, close to the shoulders. Remove the four feet.

10 Break the pelvis with a vertical stroke of a heavy knife and clean the area. Cut through the spine to remove the hind legs or 'haunch' from the loin.

11 Following the line of the backbone, cut between the legs. With the knife flat, as close to the bottom of the rib section as possible, cut the loin from the ribs.

12 With the rib section already partially opened down through the sternum or breastbone, cut down one side of the spine, to split the rib section into two.

Preparing Grey Squirrel

Now classed as vermin in Britain because of the threat it poses to the protected red squirrel, the flesh of the common grey squirrel is lean and flavoursome, due to its varied diet.

For fried dishes or cooking over coals, you'll need a younger squirrel with pliable, easily torn ears and small, sharp, white teeth. For a casserole or braise you can use a mature squirrel: with its varied diet it will have a good fat layer over the haunches and inside the cavity.

▶ *A good-sized squirrel should feed one person handsomely, two at a push.*

Tips for Cooking Squirrel

• Avoid eating squirrels taken in coniferous woods, as the flesh can be tainted by the seeds of pine cones in the animals' diet.
• As with rabbits, the removal of the squirrel's pelt is easier when the animal has just been killed.
• Slightly bitter green vegetables, like chard, kale and spring greens (collards) work well with squirrel.
• Anything containing nuts complements squirrel wonderfully.

SKINNING GREY SQUIRREL

1 As soon as is practicable, paunch the squirrel by running a knife from the sternum down to the anus. Do not cut too deeply or you may cut into the gut.

2 With the squirrel head down, allow the stomach contents to drop down slightly and pull the contents clear of the cavity. They should all come away in one go.

3 If you do not intend to cook the squirrel immediately, prop open the stomach cavity with a clean stick to encourage air circulation and cooling.

4 If you have a male, remove the testes. Try to do this with a firm, snapping type of action.

5 Then, working from the inside, locate the tail at the base of the spine and cut through it.

6 Stand firmly on the length of the tail with one foot, holding the squirrel's legs in one or both hands.

7 Lifting the squirrel up, pull slowly and steadily away from your foot, to strip the pelt back down the hind legs and towards the feet.

8 Once the hind legs are free of the skin (cut away any difficult parts near the feet), hold the body with both hands and continue to pull upwards.

9 With the squirrel now on a clean, flat surface, work the front legs clear of the skin. This isn't always the easiest part.

JOINTING SQUIRREL

1 With the head now encased in the reversed skin, remove it with one blow from a cleaver. Use a heavy knife if you wish to avoid bone fragments.

2 Remove all four feet at the nearest joint with a single blow of the cleaver. Tidy away any splinters of bone.

3 Trim away any sinews, and connective tissue. Clean away any remaining matter from the pelvis area with a damp cloth.

4 Remove the combined hind leg and loin section below the ribcage.

5 Then separate the loin from the hind legs. The 'wings' can be removed from the upper rib section if you wish.

▲ *The squirrel's combined loin and leg parts, and the rib section, are now ready for frying or braising.*

Rabbit Paella in the Field

This classic Spanish dish is often cooked outside for parties and family gatherings. It normally calls for lots of fresh shellfish, which is not often available on a hunting trip, so take frozen or canned clams or mussels with you. You will also need a large paella pan and a fire or grill big enough to support it.

Serves 6

2 rabbits, skinned and cleaned
175ml/6fl oz/¾ cup olive oil
2 medium onions, finely chopped
2 garlic cloves, sliced
1x 400g/14oz can chopped tomatoes
150g/5oz cooking chorizo, sliced
good pinch of saffron threads
500g/1¼lb/2½ cups Calasparra or
    risotto rice
12 crayfish or 275g/10oz can clams
12 live mussels or 275g/10oz can
    mussels
juice of ½ lemon
400g/14oz can chickpeas, drained
1 red (bell) pepper, finely chopped
handful of flat leaf parsley, chopped
sea salt and ground black pepper

Variations The legs of any game bird could be pre-cooked and used in place of the rabbit. You could also try squirrel in this recipe.

1 The rabbit should be pre-cooked to ensure it is tender, and to make a stock. You can do this on an open fire but a portable gas stove will give greater control. Place the whole rabbits in a pan, cover with water and add 10ml/ 2 tsp sea salt. Bring to the boil then reduce the heat to a simmer. Partially cover and cook for 40–50 minutes.

2 When the rabbit is tender and falling off the bone, remove it from the stock and allow it to cool slightly. Reserve the stock. Use your hands to pull all the meat from the bones. Set the meat aside and discard the bones.

3 Warm the paella pan on a well built-up fire. Add the oil and heat. Add the onions and cook for about 5 minutes, until softened. Add the garlic and tomatoes and cook for a further 5 minutes, stirring occasionally.

4 Add the chorizo, saffron and rice and shake the pan to mix the ingredients. Squeeze in the lemon juice and stir.

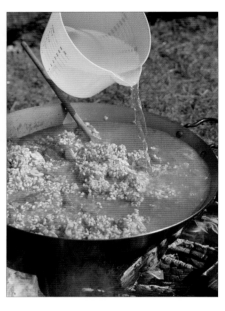

5 Add about 1.75 litres/3 pints/7½ cups of the reserved rabbit stock. Shake the pan and allow the contents to simmer gently for 15 minutes.

6 Add the rabbit meat, chickpeas and shellfish. Sprinkle the chopped parsley and red pepper over the top and crack plenty of black pepper over.

7 Simmer the paella for approximately 5 minutes more, then test the rice to make sure it is completely cooked.

8 Turn off the heat and leave the paella to sit for 5 minutes so the rice has time to fully expand and absorb all the stock, then stir through. Serve with a large glass of Rioja.

Energy 857kcal/3584kJ; Protein 57.8g; Carbohydrate 88.1g, of which sugars 9.2g; Fat 30.4g, of which saturates 6.3g; Cholesterol 177mg; Calcium 171mg; Fibre 5g; Sodium 824mg

Fire-braised Rabbit in Cider

While out hunting you might find the opportunity to gather some of nature's harvest. In the right season, wild mushrooms can be found in the fields or woods and are a natural partner to all game. Be sure to pick only those you can positively identify, and if you are unsure take some dried mushrooms on your hunt. For this recipe you will need a frying pan, a heavy pan with a lid and a slow-burning fire.

Serves 2

1 medium or large rabbit, skinned
   and cleaned
30ml/2 tbsp olive oil or
   50g/2oz/4 tbsp lard
1 large onion, peeled and sliced
225g/8oz fresh mushrooms, sliced, or
   50g/2oz dried mushrooms soaked in
   300ml/½ pint/1¼ cups hot water
2 garlic cloves, peeled and sliced
600ml/1 pint/2½ cups medium (hard)
   cider or apple juice
any wild herbs such as sage,
   marjoram, bay or thyme
sea salt and ground black pepper

1 Joint the rabbit by cutting the legs from the body, and then cutting the saddle into four across its length. Discard the carcass.

2 Heat a frying pan and add the oil or fat. Season the rabbit pieces and brown on all sides. Transfer to a heavy pan and return the frying pan to the heat.

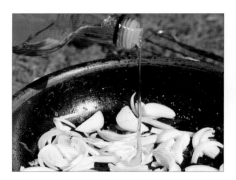

3 Add the onions to the frying pan, with a little more olive oil if necessary, and cook, stirring, for 4–5 minutes or until they are soft and beginning to brown.

4 Add the mushrooms and garlic to the frying pan. Cook for a further 2 minutes.

5 When the mushrooms are golden brown, pour in the cider. Bring to the boil, reduce the heat and simmer for 5 minutes. Add more salt and pepper, any herbs you may have collected and either 300ml/½ pint/1¼ cups water or the liquor from the dried mushrooms.

6 Transfer the contents of the frying pan to the heavy pan and place over the heat. Bring to the boil again, cover the pan and simmer for 30 minutes.

7 After 30 minutes stir the contents of the pan. If it is low on liquid, add a little more cider or water; if it is watery continue the cooking with the lid partly off. Cook for a further 20–30 minutes, or until the meat from the hind legs leaves the bone. Serve with crusty bread.

Variation The rabbit could be replaced with pheasant legs or jointed squirrel.

Energy 571kcal/2401kJ; Protein 58.1g; Carbohydrate 42g, of which sugars 38.4g; Fat 20.3g, of which saturates 5.9g; Cholesterol 208mg; Calcium 163mg; Fibre 3.4g; Sodium 140mg

Hare Cooked with White Beans

This recipe uses the loin of hare, which is a wonderfully tender and tasty piece of meat, not dissimilar to a small beef fillet. This all-in-one dish needs only a deep frying pan to cook it and can be quickly made on a portable gas stove or a fire. You could also cook venison fillet steak in the same way.

Serves 2

2 saddles of hare
50g/2oz/4 tbsp lard or dripping
1 medium onion, diced
2 garlic cloves, diced
225g/8oz wild mushrooms, sliced
150ml/¼ pint/⅔ cup Marsala wine
400g/14oz can cannellini
   beans, drained
175g/6oz cavolo nero (or other dark
   leafy greens), shredded
any available herbs
sea salt and ground black pepper

1 Remove the loins from the saddle by cutting down either side of the spine, as close to it as possible; turn the knife away from the spine, and, using the ribs to guide you, cut the meat away from the bone.

2 Remove the sinewy skin from the loins. Lay each one on a board, sinew side down, and position your blade at the tail end of the loin, flat to the board. Slide the blade towards the top.

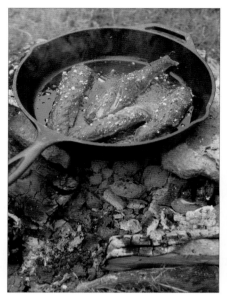

3 Heat the pan and add half the fat. Season the loins with salt and pepper and when the fat is sizzling add them to the pan and cook quickly on all sides to seal the meat. Remove from the pan and reserve.

4 Add the rest of the fat to the pan, then add the onions and cook until softened, stirring occasionally. Add the garlic and cook for 1 minute.

5 Add the sliced mushrooms to the pan and cook until just softening.

Variation Diced venison or boar loin (which requires longer cooking), or the breast meat of game birds can also be used in this recipe.

6 Pour the Marsala into the pan and bubble quickly to reduce by half – this will intensify its sweetness.

7 Add the drained beans, shredded cavolo nero, some additional salt and pepper and any herbs you may have available. Bring the pan to the boil, reduce the heat and simmer.

8 When the cabbage is soft and tender, slice the hare loins across their length into bitesize pieces. Add them to the pan and stir in. Remove the pan from the heat and leave to sit for 3–5 minutes to allow the pieces of hare to heat through before serving.

Energy 1050kcal/4403kJ; Protein 109.2g; Carbohydrate 40.6g, of which sugars 13g; Fat 51.3g, of which saturates 10.5g; Cholesterol 23mg; Calcium 255mg; Fibre 15.1g; Sodium 868mg

Fire-braised Hare with Burgundy

The meat of the hare is rich and full of flavour, and a match for even the most robust of wines. Burgundy will give a real depth to the gravy, which is finished with chestnuts to sweeten the dish. This recipe is good for using up the legs of the hare when you have used the loin in another dish; there won't be much meat but the flavour packs a real punch.

Serves 2

50g/2oz/4 tbsp lard or 30ml/2 tbsp olive oil
2 hind legs and 2 front legs of hare
1 large onion, peeled and diced
2 carrots, diced
4 garlic cloves, sliced, with a handful of chopped wild garlic (see Cook's tip)
115g/4oz Bayonne ham (from the knuckle), diced
300ml/½ pint/1¼ cups red Burgundy
1 chicken stock (bouillon) cube
1 bay leaf
350g/12oz waxy potatoes, diced
200g/7oz vacuum-packed chestnuts
1 small Savoy or other green cabbage
50g/2oz/¼ cup butter
sea salt and ground black pepper

Variation You can also use diced wild goat or venison shoulder for this recipe, but extend the cooking time by 30 minutes before adding the potatoes.

1 Heat the pan and add the fat or oil. Season the hare legs with salt and pepper and place in the pan together with the onion and carrot. Fry over high heat, stirring frequently, to colour.

2 Add the garlic and ham to the pan and cook until softened.

3 Pour the wine into the pan and allow it to bubble. Crumble the stock cube in to the pan, together with the bay leaf, salt and pepper and 450ml/¾ pint/scant 2 cups water. Move the pan to a cooler part of the fire, so the heat is low but steady. Cover and cook for 1 hour.

4 Stir occasionally and check that the casserole is not becoming too dry: if necessary add a little more water. After 1 hour add the potatoes, replace the lid and cook for a further 15 minutes.

Cook's tip Wild garlic grows in profusion in damp, shady places in spring and makes a lovely addition to many game recipes, especially when you're cooking in the field. Adding chopped leaves and bulbs to this recipe and then sprinkling the flowers over the top of the finished dish will give extra flavour and visual appeal.

5 Next add the chestnuts. Replace the lid once more and cook for a final 5 minutes. Taste and adjust the seasoning if necessary.

6 Around 10 minutes before you are ready to eat, rinse the shredded cabbage and put in a pan with a knob of butter, salt and pepper.

7 Place over the fire and cook for 3–4 minutes, stirring now and then, until any water has evaporated and the cabbage is lightly cooked and coated in butter. Serve with the hare.

Energy 1058kcal/4418kJ; Protein 78.8g; Carbohydrate 52.3g, of which sugars 22.8g; Fat 49.5g, of which saturates 18.4g; Cholesterol 100mg; Calcium 219mg; Fibre 8.6g; Sodium 1012mg

Nutty Squirrel in the Field

The flavours of Austria are combined here to lift that of the squirrel: smoky ham, sweet wine and caraway seeds will transport you straight to the south Tyrolean mountains. This slow-cooked dish will require a pot with a well-fitting lid, and can be cooked either on a fire or on a portable stove. The handful of hazelnuts added at the end reflects the squirrel's diet and finishes the dish perfectly.

Serves 2

50g/2oz/4 tbsp lard or beef dripping
2 large onions, sliced
175g/6oz Tyrolean ham, diced
5ml/1 tsp caraway seeds
2 squirrels, skinned, gutted, cleaned
   and quartered
300ml/½ pint/1¼ cups sweet white
   wine such as Gewürtztraminer
50g/2oz hazelnuts, toasted, skinned
   and roughly chopped
sea salt and ground black pepper

Variations You could also use rabbit or pheasant for this recipe – in which case cook for just 45 minutes in total – or boar or goat, which will need around the same cooking time as the squirrel.

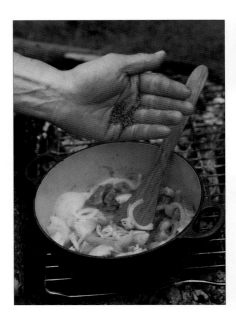

1 Warm the pan, add the fat and fry the onions and ham gently until the onions have softened. Season with salt and pepper, then add the caraway seeds.

2 Add the squirrel pieces to the pan, and stir to coat with fat and combine with the onions and ham.

3 Pour in the wine together with 400ml/14fl oz/1⅔ cups water and bring the liquid to a simmer.

4 Cover the pan. If the lid does not fit tightly, adding a layer of foil will help to keep the heat and moisture inside. Move the pan to a cooler part of the fire and cook gently for 1–1½ hours.

5 At the end of the cooking time, remove the lid and check the meat. If it is still a little tough, leave to simmer gently until it leaves the bone, adding more water if necessary.

6 When the meat is ready, finish by adding the chopped hazelnuts and serve immediately.

Cook's tip If your pan lid doesn't fit well you can seal it with a flour and water paste, which as it hardens will create the same effect inside the pan as a pressure cooker. Use 450g/1lb/4 cups plain (all-purpose) flour and enough water to create a pliable dough. Mix in a plastic bag and stick the dough around the lip of the pan before pressing on the lid.

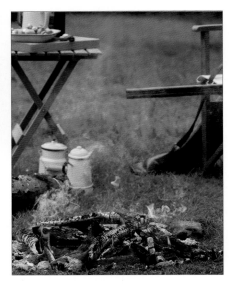

Energy 803kcal/3344kJ; Protein 48.4g; Carbohydrate 19.3g, of which sugars 16.5g; Fat 47.7g, of which saturates 13.6g; Cholesterol 128mg; Calcium 100mg; Fibre 3g; Sodium 1165mg.

Squirrel Braised Outside

This recipe juggles sweet and sour flavours to perk up the squirrel meat. Many cultures around the world blend these two opposites, but the use of wine vinegar derives from ancient Roman times.

Serves 2

50g/2oz/4 tbsp lard or dripping
  or olive oil
1 large onion, roughly chopped
2 carrots, roughly chopped
2 celery sticks, roughly chopped
2 squirrels, cleaned and quartered
4 garlic cloves, peeled
2 bushy sprigs rosemary or oregano
1 cinnamon stick
30ml/2 tbsp red wine vinegar
60ml/4 tbsp red wine
50g/2oz/⅓ cup raisins
10ml/2 tsp black treacle (molasses)
sea salt and ground black pepper

3 Add the garlic, herbs and cinnamon and cook for 4–5 minutes. Then add the vinegar, together with the red wine and enough water to cover the meat. Season, cover the pan, and simmer for 1¼ hours, topping up with more water if necessary.

4 After 1¼ hours add the raisins and treacle. Replace the lid and cook for a further 30 minutes, after which the squirrel should be tender.

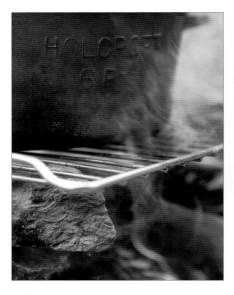

1 Warm a large heavy casserole over high heat. Add the fat or oil, and when it is hot add the chopped onion, carrot and celery. Fry, stirring, for 2–3 minutes.

2 Season the squirrel with salt and pepper and add the pieces to the pan. Cook for 5–8 minutes, turning the meat to colour the pieces on all sides.

Energy 571kcal/2385kJ; Protein 35.3g; Carbohydrate 36.9g, of which sugars 34.1g; Fat 30.2g, of which saturates 11.8g; Cholesterol 88mg; Calcium 116mg; Fibre 4.7g; Sodium 178mg

Useful Addresses

BUTCHERS' SUPPLIERS
UK
J Adams Ltd
124 Scotland Street
Sheffield S3 7DE
Tel: 011 427 23612
Email: sales@sheffieldknives.co.uk
www.sheffieldknives.co.uk

Butchers Sundries Direct
Unit 11, Repton Court
Repton Close, Burnt Mills
Basildon SS13 1LN
Tel: 01268 270995
www.butcherssundriesdirect.co.uk

Scobie & Junior Ltd
1 Singer Road
East Kilbride, Glasgow,
Scotland G75 0XS
www.scobiesdirect.com

USA
PRO-CUTLERY
8974 Route 32, Freehold,
New York (NY), 12431,
Tel: +518 634 2240
www.procutlery.com

Southern Indiana Butcher Supply
PO Box 34, Lamar, IN 47550
Tel: 812-529-8456
www.butchersupply.net

Cutlery And More
135 Prairie Lake Rd.
East Dundee, IL 60118
Tel: 1-800-650-9866 (toll free)
www.CutleryAndMore.com

CANADA
Canada Cutlery Inc
1964 Notion Road
Pickering ON, L1V 2G3
Tel: 1.800.698.8277 (toll free)
www.canadacutlery.com

AUSTRALIA
Vadals
12 Container Street
Tingalpa, Queensland
Australia 4173
Tel: 07 3907 7878
www.vadals.com.au

GAME DEALERS AND
SPECIALIST BUTCHERS
UK
William Rose Butchers
126 Lordship Lane, Dulwich
London, SE22 8HD
Tel: 020 86939191
www.williamrosebutchers.com

Teesdale Game & Poultry
Durham Indoor Market
Market Place, Durham, DH1 3NJ
Tel: 0191 3750664
www.teesdalegame.co.uk

Blackmoor Game Ltd
Wield Wood Farm
Upper Wield, Alresford
Hampshire, SO24 9RU
Tel: 01420 563831
www.blackmoorgame.co.uk

Round Green Deer Farm
Round Green Lane, Worsbrough
Barnsley, S75 3DR
Tel: 01226 205577
www.roundgreenfarm.co.uk

Willo Game
Shuttocks Wood, Norbury
Nr Bishops Castle
Shropshire, SY9 5EA
Tel: 01588 650539

www.willogame.co.uk
Macbeth's
11 Tolbooth Street, Forres, Moray
Scotland, IV36 1PH

Tel: 01309 672254
www.macbeths.com

Campbells Prime Meat Ltd
The Heatherfield
Haining Road
Lathallen (By Linlithgow)
Edinburgh, EH49 6LQ
www.campbellsmeat.com

Carmarthenshire & Wales Game Farm
Cwmgelli Fach, Llanfynydd
Carmarthen, SA32 7TR
Tel: 01558 668491

USA
Elk USA
Grande Natural Meat
PO Box 10, Del Norte, Colorado 81132
Tel: 1-888-338-4581
www.elkusa.com

Venison America
494 County Road A, Hudson, WI 54016
Tel: (800) 310 2360
www.venisonamerica.com

Broken Arrow Ranch
3296 Junction Highway
Ingram, TX 78025
Tel: (800) 962-4263
www.brokenarrowranch.com

Cowboy Free Range Meat
P.O. Box 8549
1655 Berger Lane, Jackson Hole,
Wyoming
Tel: Toll-Free: 1-866-435-5411,
www.cowboyfreerangemeat.com

CANADA
Black Angus Meat
740 Lakeshore Road East
Mississauga, Ontario, L5G 1M5
Tel: (905) 271-2333
www.blackangusmeat.com

AUSTRALIA
Naturally Australian Meat & Game Ltd
5 Shoebury Street
Rocklea, Queensland
Tel: 61 7 3848 0054
www.namag.com.au

Index

ACKNOWLEDGEMENTS

Robert and Jake would like
to thank Kate and Lou for
their unswerving love and
support during this lengthy
but fun project, as well as
their parents and families.
They would also like to thank
the people who have helped
make this book possible;
Michael Cannon of the
Wemmergill Estate, Anne
Smyth, Nicola and Stephen
Crouch at Hampshire Game,
Derek Sealy at Wiltshire
Game Ltd, The Cranborne
Estate, Richard Squires, John
Massey, Tom & Mark at
Angel Cottage Farm,
Matthew & Katie Fry, Ben &
Lindy, *The Shooting Gazette*,
Fieldsports Magazine,
Schoffel Countrywear, Coen
& Catherine Stork at Chateau
de Villette. Joanne Rippin
and the team at Anness
Publishing, Andy Parle for his
great recipes and Fergal
Connolly for his brilliant food
styling in the field and studio.
    Our warmest and deepest
thanks go to Ray Smith
whose talent, warmth and
huge willingness to share his
quite staggering depth of
knowledge. Ray and Mary,
his wife, really live the rural
idyll – they are our inspiration.
Many, many thanks.